D1585389

# NO-FUSS VEGETARIAN COOKING

# NO-FUSS VEGETARIAN COOKING

## Quick and easy ideas for meat-free meals

## SARAH BROWN

**EBURY PRESS**
**LONDON**

*To Brian and Sheila Street*

First published in 1998

1 2 3 4 5 6 7 8 9 10

First published in the United Kingdom in 1998 by Ebury Press
Random House, 20 Vauxhall Bridge Road, London SW1V 2SA

Random House Australia (Pty) Limited
20 Alfred Street, Milsons Point, Sydney,
New South Wales 2061, Australia

Random House New Zealand Limited
18 Poland Road, Glenfield, Auckland 10, New Zealand

Random House South Africa (Pty) Limited
Endulini, 5a Jubilee Road, Parktown 2193, South Africa

Random House UK Limited Reg. No. 954009

Papers used by Ebury Press are natural, recyclable products made from wood grown in sustainable forests.

A CIP catalogue record for this book is available from the British Library.

ISBN 0 09 186320 1

Text design by Ruth Prentice
Jacket design by the Senate
Photography by Jean Cazals
Styling by Roísín Nield
Food stylist Marie-Ange Lapierre

Printed and bound in Singapore by Tien Wah Press

# CONTENTS

# ACKNOWLEDGEMENTS

Thanks to Nick Cressey for making days of testing recipes such fun. Also thanks to Elisabeth Brown, Anne May, Rachel Hall and Joanne Tracy for some great recipe ideas and particularly Dan Schlesinger for introducing me to some marvellous Japanese ingredients. I am greatly indebted to John Crawford for all his help with the notes on food and wine.

At Ebury Press, I would like to thank Fiona MacIntyre, who has shown so much enthusiasm for my ideas from the outset, and Penny Simpson for her patient and thorough editing.

Finally, thanks to my family, Paul, Ralph and Greg.

# INTRODUCTION

MANY PEOPLE WANT TO EAT LESS MEAT these days for all sorts of reasons – health, food scares, allergies or concern for animal welfare. But what no one wants is to spend hours shopping or ages in the kitchen. I've written this book for all those who, like me, want to eat good vegetarian food but don't want to feel that it will take an enormous amount of effort.

When I first started writing vegetarian recipes, my main concern was to reassure people that they could have a highly nutritious diet without eating meat or fish. I also wanted to blur the distinction between meat meals and meat-free meals, so that vegetarian fare could be seen as entirely acceptable mainstream food. Whilst many people now readily eat meat-free meals, one of the remaining myths of vegetarian cookery is that cooking without meat is somehow more trouble. I hope this book will dispel that myth.

I have always written from personal experience, and at the time of writing I have two small children. So, like many others, I am juggling both a career and parenthood as well as wanting time for numerous other interests. My recipes are by necessity simple and speedy. True, I have now had twenty years of experience cooking this sort of food, but many changes in the last decade or so have made getting and preparing good food easier. For example, most large supermarkets stock an excellent range of vegetarian basics plus a huge selection of fruit and vegetables. Even specialist ingredients are no longer so hard to find.

What goes with what is a frequent question. To take some of the headache out of this, I've written some notes about both meal- and menu-planning as well as suggestions about what to drink with it all. I haven't given separate menus or recipes specifically for children, but have included some notes on dietary requirements and tips on how to avoid battles over food.

In the next few pages you'll find advice on planning a good storecupboard, time-saving tips and notes on useful gadgets, both big and small. There are tips on choosing an appropriate cooking technique to fit into your schedule. Finally, there is some information about some of the meat substitutes available, to help solve the 'fast food' dilemma as well as acting as a bridge between eating and not eating meat.

Following the introductory section, you'll find the recipes. There are chapters on familiar types of dishes, such as soups and desserts, and also chapters of recipes for particular situations and busy lifestyles. Many of the recipes include serving suggestions or suggestions on how to put several dishes together to make a meal. Most of the recipes serve four people; the few exceptions are for those worth cooking in a larger quantity or more suitable to cook in a smaller amount. Recipes are also coded with the following:

♦ gluten free

♦ sugar free

♦ nut free

♦ dairy free

♦ suitable for freezing

Gluten free recipes are free of all main sources of wheat, including soy sauce, but you should check products such as mustard and baking powder, where certain brands contain gluten.

Sugar free means the recipe has no added sugar, but it may contain ingredients with a sugar content, such as apple juice.

Nut free means the recipe is free of nuts and nut oils, as well as sesame and sesame oil, but may contain other seeds such as sunflower or pumpkin seeds and their corresponding oils.

Dairy free means that the recipe contains no dariy products or eggs.

Suitable for freezing means that the dish can be frozen generally for at least a month, in many cases longer – consult your freezer handbook.

Throughout the book you'll find extra tips, on cooking techniques, and what to look for when buying and storing less familiar ingredients.

I hope the recipes and advice will help you discover how easy and simple vegetarian food can be to prepare. After all, if it has been no fuss to assemble, you'll find it even more enjoyable.

## PLANNING MENUS AND MEALS

Thinking about an individual recipe is one thing, but planning what to serve with it, or putting together a menu with several courses, can be daunting. With familiarity and practice you develop a sense of what works with what, but if you are new to vegetarian cooking, these five simple tips will help take the hassle out of the planning.

**1 Feature a different ingredient in each dish** The bonus, and yet also the difficulty, with vegetarian food is that so many ingredients can work well in lots of different circumstances. For example, almonds could be used in a dressing or soup, in a starter, in a main dish such as a classic nut roast or as a filling for a pie and, equally well, in a pudding. This sort of crossover doesn't occur as frequently in an omnivorous diet – if you chose a starter of fish, you probably would not think of having fish as the main course. Fish is also unlikely to turn up on the pudding trolley.

**2 Get a balance between heavy and light** It's important to avoid overusing the same type of ingredient in each dish: a carbohydrate-loaded meal of rice-stuffed pancakes served with potato would be very hard work! At the other end of the scale, a salad starter followed by a vegetable sauté and then a fruit salad may all be very colourful, but it would not be a satisfying meal, and it also needs a lot of preparation.

**3 Include a good selection of colours** Despite its bad 'brown' image, which is quite unjustified, vegetarian food can be very colourful. Try to imagine what might stand out when planning meals. Don't serve a green vegetable with a predominantly green main course, or a side dish of carrots with a main course of red lentils. Greens and browns are complementary. Tomato sauce always adds a splash of colour, especially to a burger/potato plate which can look rather brown. If your casserole looks a little dull, add a dollop of yoghurt or some freshly chopped herbs.

**4 Aim for different textures** There are all sorts of textures in vegetarian food, from chewy rice to smooth soup, soft pâté to a crunchy stir-fry. Try to make sure that your meal includes a good variety. For example, a stew doesn't work well following a soup. Raw ingredients always provide a textural contrast for a cooked dish.

**5 Don't feel you have to stick to conventional ways of serving meals** There are quite a few dishes, such as lasagne or a substantial salad, which really don't need an accompaniment. If you make a vegetable stew you probably won't need an extra vegetable with it, although you might want a carbohydrate such as rice, potato or bread. Serving several small dishes together can make a delicious and satisfying meal, and each guest can select his or her own plateful.

**EVERYDAY NUTRITION TIPS**
◆ On the whole, if you plan meals based on a variety of ingredients and incorporating different textures and colours, you are likely to end up with a good nutritional balance too.
◆ Think of the staples of vegetarian food in four groups: dairy products (including eggs), grains, pulses (beans and lentils), and nuts and seeds. As long as you make combinations of two or more groups each day, preferably at the same

meal, you will be getting first-class protein. Try not to include too much from the dairy group as these foods are high in fats.
◆ As well as the staple foods, eat as much fruit and vegetables as possible because they provide vital vitamins and minerals. The simplest rule of thumb is to try to eat a minimum of five different helpings, either raw or cooked.
◆ It is good to get energy (calories) from unrefined grains.

**COOKING FOR ONE OR TWO**
◆ Lots of recipes can be adapted for smaller numbers. It is little trouble to prepare a small amount of pasta or couscous.
◆ Stir-fry dishes can easily be scaled down for one or two.
◆ Salads are ideal to make in small quantities, although dressings can be more of a problem. However, many dressings, such as Classic Vinaigrette (page 00), can be made in large amounts and kept for days.
◆ Filo pastry sheets make good individual pies, without the need to make lots of pastry.
◆ Sauces, soups and casseroles all freeze well. Make plenty and then freeze in suitable-sized portions. Ring the changes on eating the same dish by varying the accompaniments.

**ENTERTAINING**
◆ Unless it is an impromptu meal, don't try to do everything on the day. Many dishes, especially soups, stews and sauces, are better cooked the day before and reheated. Alternatively, make use of the freezer.

◆ An alternative to a formal meal is to offer two or three tasty snacks supplemented with cheese, breads and bought pâtés such as humus.

◆ In the summer try a barbecue where you can cook to order.

◆ Keep a well-stocked storecupboard ready for unexpected visitors.

## A VEGETARIAN DIET FOR CHILDREN

For a variety of reasons, many children don't want to eat meat. This may happen as soon as they start on solids, or later as they become more aware of animals. Or you may have to alter your child's diet because you discover that he or she has an allergy or a bad reaction to certain foods. There should be no reason for a child who is not eating meat or fish to be less healthy than one who is. I say 'should' because much depends on what sort of meat-free diet it is – a 'vegetarian' diet consisting just of fizzy drinks and sweets would, of course, be of little nutritional value.

In general, the same rules that adults should follow for healthy eating apply to children too:

◆ lots of unrefined carbohydrates such as cereals, grains and wholemeal bread

◆ plenty of vegetables and fruit, both raw and cooked

◆ fats are important for children, and their calories are useful too. However, as with adults, don't make fats the main source of energy.

Protein is essential for growth and thus obviously vital for children. Make sure your child eats plenty of wholemeal cereals and bread, some pulses, such as baked beans or humus, nuts and dairy products on a daily basis. First-class protein is found in dairy products and eggs, but also in combinations of food groups such as pulses and grains, or nuts and grains. Beans on toast is a classic example of a first-class protein combination, as is a cashew pilaff or a lentil pie.

Children need smaller quantities of all the vitamins and minerals that adults need, except calcium: the recommended daily allowance for children is 600 mg (for adults it is 500 mg). Good sources of calcium are full-fat milk and dairy products, tofu and calcium-enriched soya milk, nuts and seeds. I think balance and variety are the key words – if your child eats lots of different things you shouldn't need to feel worried as to whether he is getting all the nutrients he needs.

So here we have this perfect child sitting down to muesli and wholemeal toast for breakfast; peanut butter cheese rolls, salad and fruit at lunch time; and a plate of spaghetti with lentil and tomato sauce and green vegetables at tea. If only.... I have one child who will eat virtually any vegetable, and who is very willing to have a go at new foods. My other child is much fussier. Here are some tips if, like me, you sometimes have difficulties with your children over food:

◆ if your child won't eat main meals, make sure snacks are good value: offer toast or bread instead of biscuits and cake

◆ build up on good foods that they do like. For example, cereals such as muesli can be eaten just as well at tea time as in the morning

◆ serve vegetables in different ways to make them more appealing. A child may prefer a raw carrot to a cooked one. Finely grate vegetables into rice dishes or a burger to disguise them.

◆ if your child is allergic to cow's milk, try goat's milk or a calcium-enriched soya milk

◆ try some of the non-meat fast foods to compete with burgers and sausages

◆ suggest fruit, nuts or dried fruits instead of sweets. Dried fruits are useful sources of minerals as well as being appealingly sweet

◆ try and involve children in cooking: they may be prepared to try something different if they have made it themselves

## TEENAGE VEGETARIANS

You may have picked up this book because one member of your family has decided to become vegetarian, and you want to find fuss-free food for them that will also suit the rest of your family. The chances are that the one member is 1) a teenager and 2) a girl. Statistics show that the biggest group claiming not to eat meat are women between the ages of 16 and 24. In general, you shouldn't worry if your teenage child wants to become vegetarian. A well-balanced, varied vegetarian diet should provide all that an adolescent needs for growth. But whilst getting enough of the major nutrients, such as protein, carbohydrate and fats, shouldn't be a problem, it is important to remember the minor nutrients that are just as vital, namely iron and calcium.

Lack of iron over a long period can cause anaemia. Meat, particularly offal, is a good source of iron, so if meat is cut out of the diet, the iron has to come from somewhere else. For vegetarians, good sources of iron are green leafy vegetables, pulses, tofu and dried fruits. Many breakfast cereals are also fortified with iron. Remember that more iron will be absorbed by the body if these foods are eaten in conjunction with those that contain Vitamin C, so be sure to include lots of fresh fruits and vegetables such as oranges and peppers in the meal-planning.

It is important for teenagers to get plenty of calcium in their diet. Calcium is accumulated in the bones during the teenage years and this can help prevent the onset of osteoporosis later in life. Good sources of calcium are full-fat milk and cheese, nuts, dark green leafy vegetables, sesame seeds and sesame products such as tahini, and sunflower seeds. If your teenager wants to be vegan (i.e., eating no dairy products at all) it is vital to use calcium-enriched soya products (milk, yoghurt, cheese and tofu).

One reason many teenagers turn to vegetarianism is to lose weight. This in itself is not necessarily harmful and you shouldn't panic. However, vegetarianism and the associated cutting out of foods may be a sign of something more serious such as an eating disorder. If you are at all worried then you should seek professional help as soon as possible because the earlier these conditions are picked up, the more easily they can be treated.

Finally, don't feel that you will be sentenced to a life of preparing two entirely separate menus every mealtime. Whilst at first you may have to spend a bit of time scrutinising lists of ingredients on packets, you'll soon find that you get to know what is available. Supermarkets are now much more helpful and label products where necessary as suitable for vegetarians. You may have to buy some new ingredients, such as tahini or tofu, but lots of the staples fundamental to a vegetarian diet will be familiar, such as rice, pasta or pota-toes. Many meals can be prepared using these and adding meat or extra vegetarian protein at a later stage or serving it separately.

**THE WELL-STOCKED STORECUPBOARD**
Do you ever look in your refrigerator and find an onion, a few mushrooms or perhaps a pepper, some carrots, maybe an egg or a bit of cheese, and then wonder where the next meal is coming from? Having a well-stocked storecupboard really helps on days like this. Even those few items can be the basis for several interesting meals, as long as you've got back-up staples such as flour, grains or pasta, a decent oil and a tin of tomatoes. With these you could make pasta with a quick sauce, a risotto or a simple pizza.

This storecupboard list isn't meant to be definitive, but more of a check list to ensure you have some of the most useful items. Look, too, in the chapter introductions where I've described a few more unusual ingredients. Just remember occasionally to check on your stocks, to top them up and replace any past their 'best-before' dates:

**Storecupboard items:**
CONCENTRATED APPLE JUICE; DRIED FRUITS: apricots, sultanas etc; DRIED MUSHROOMS; FLAVOURINGS: soy sauce, dried herbs and spices; FLOUR: gram, wholemeal, white; GRAINS: basmati rice, long-grain rice, bulgar wheat, couscous, maize flour (corn meal); NUTS: cashews, hazelnuts, almonds, walnuts; OILS: olive oil, sunflower oil, sesame oil; PASTA: a variety of shapes, including lasagne; PULSES:

split red lentils, Puy lentils, tins of beans and chick peas; SEEDS: sesame seeds, sunflower seeds, tahini; SILKEN TOFU; TINNED VEGETABLES: artichokes, olives; TOMATOES: tinned, passata, sun-dried; WINE

**Useful perishables for the refrigerator:**
CHEESE; hard and soft; CRÈME FRAÎCHE; EGGS; GARLIC; PLAIN YOGHURT; REGULAR TOFU

**Basic vegetables and fruit that keep well:**
CARROTS and other root vegetables; LEMONS and other citrus fruits; ONIONS; POTATOES; SQUASH

**Useful freezer back-ups:**
BUTTER; FILO PASTRY; QUORN

**TIME-SAVING TIPS**
Saving time is part of the rationale behind *No-Fuss Vegetarian Cooking*.Here are a few tips, most of which are really commonsense reminders.

Time-saving begins with **shopping**. A very short, sharp shopping list keeps me focussed, and I rarely come out of the shop with extras. Also, I find it helps to have a good stock of basics at home so that I am only left with essential perish-ables to buy.

There are three things that help make the **preparation** of food seem less effort and there-fore quicker: 1) the right equipment, 2) having the ingredients to hand and 3) having a sense of how you are going to organise the dish.
◆ any equipment you intend to use should be to hand, not at the back of a cupboard
◆ use a food processor for preparing large quantities, and freeze extra portions
◆ a hand-held electric mixer is useful for cake mixtures and batters

◆ a blender gets sauces and soups very smooth in an instant

◆ a small electric grinder or mill is good for breadcrumbs, nuts and herbs

◆ keep your knives sharp, and have a decent sized chopping board

◆ have a bowl or bag handy for collecting all the vegetable peelings and trimmings as you go along. This saves time clearing up and also keeps the work surface clearer

◆ use reusable baking paper to line roasting tins and baking trays. This saves washing up

◆ make use of a microwave for cooking vegetables quickly and for thawing frozen food

◆ the following are worth having: sturdy garlic press; good-sized pastry brush; effective peeler; kitchen scissors; ginger grater; lemon zester

◆ for a stir-fry everything should be ready prepared before you begin to cook; otherwise while one thing is cooking, be preparing the next

◆ if planning meals with several courses think through what can be done in advance and what jobs can be dovetailed together

When you want to save time, you should choose **techniques** that suit your schedule.

◆ stir-frying and sautéing produce quick colourful vegetable dishes

◆ oven roasting takes longer, but leaves you free to do other things, even to eat a starter whilst the food is cooking

◆ casseroles may be slow, but after preparation taking only 15 minutes or less they need very little attention

◆ lasagne can be speeded up by using no-cook pasta and my Easy Tomato Sauce (page 98).

## Ten Quick Tips

**1** Bread and 'instant' couscous are the quickest of carbohydrates to bulk out a meal.

**2** Dress fresh pasta with butter and chopped herbs, or noodles with soy sauce and sesame oil for a simple meal.

**3** Rub a pan with garlic before cooking to add flavour.

**4** Use crème fraîche or melted soft goat's cheese to make rich instant sauces.

**5** A handful of nuts or grated cheese will add instant protein.

**6** Buy ready-washed and trimmed salad in bags – the time saved justifies the extra cost.

**7** Drizzle a good olive oil on to a salad if you have no dressing prepared.

**8** Serve fruit as a starter or dessert.

**9** Remember that two or three small dishes put together can make a satisfying meal.

**10** Look in the chapters on Express Eating, Cooker-Top Quickies and Pasta for fast meals.

## ORGANIC FOOD

Like many cooks, I am concerned about the quality and origins of the ingredients that I use. Some years ago when the spotlight was first turned on intensive farming, I began to look for alternatives. They weren't easy to find. Today, however, it is a boom time for 'going organic', and there is an ever-increasing range of food available. But what is organic food, and is it worth the extra it costs?

In the United Kingdom, organically grown foods are regulated by the UK Register of Organic Food Standards. By law the food should be certified by a recognised body, such as the Soil Association or the

British Organic Farmers and Growers: look for their marks when buying. Anything sold as organic must be produced in a way that avoids the use of artificial pesticides and fertilisers. Organic farmers concentrate on conserving and enhancing the fertility of the soil by natural methods such as crop rotation. Organic producers also try to preserve natural habitats and pay attention to environmental concerns.

Nowadays most major supermarkets sell a range of organic foods. Look out too for local schemes such as box deliveries. For a fixed price you receive a weekly (or fortnightly) box of fresh produce, with potatoes, eggs and some other non-perishable organic items sold separately. The produce should be locally grown and therefore fresh. These boxes are fun to have if you are prepared for the unexpected.

It is possible to buy organic milk and dairy products, organically grown grains and bi-products such as flour or pasta. There are also organically grown dried fruits, seeds, nuts and pulses, and canned organic baked beans.

Research has shown that organic foods are more nutritious than conventionally grown foods, being higher in some vitamins and trace elements. This may be due to the fact that organic crops take longer to grow and contain less water. Genetically modified organisms (GMOs) are rapidly finding their way into the food chain. As yet it is impossible to judge the consequences of their effects on us and the environment, but eating organic food is a sure way of avoiding them.

Sadly, organic food is, on the whole, more expensive than food grown by conventional means. To avoid wastage, bear in mind that fresh organic produce doesn't last as long as conventionally grown vegetables and fruits – organic apples in a fruit bowl may end up like cotton wool in just a few days.

Because of the price and the word 'organic', we have an expectation that everything labelled as such will have a vastly superior flavour. Whilst in some instances this is true, particularly of a crop such as carrots, with other foods the difference is minimal. It is obviously a bonus if the food does taste much better, but this is not the main criterion for 'going organic'.

## MEAT SUBSTITUTES

Why, you may ask, if you are vegetarian, should you want to eat something that is designed to look or taste like meat? In fact, there are numerous reasons why people choose not to eat meat. They may have an allergic reaction to it; they may believe that a meat-free diet is healthier or cheaper; or they may prefer the imitation to the real thing. Those new to a vegetarian diet often like to have a recognisable bridge between the food they were used to eating and the food they want to switch to, and they still want to enjoy favourite traditional dishes. Hence the appeal of making something like Shepherd's Pie with a substitute mince rather than the real thing.

When I first became a vegetarian, the main meat substitute was **TVP**, or textured vegetable protein. It was usually sold in a dehydrated form, as either chunks or mince, and was often heavily flavoured with yeast extract. There were also tinned varieties, equivalent to tins of stewing steak or mince. These are all of nutritional value and can work well when making traditional meat dishes such as stews or recipes based on mince, but I must admit that I never found them very appealing and instead based my cooking on non-processed vegetarian staples such as grains and pulses. Meat substitutes similar to these are still available today, but there are now also two widely available products that can act as meat substitutes – tofu and Quorn. They are used to make some of the fast foods mentioned below, but I find they are also an inspiration in their own right.

**Tofu** is a virtually tasteless, creamy-coloured food made from soya beans. It is high in protein, low in fat and cholesterol-free. It is also a good source of calcium. So-called 'firm' or regular tofu can be sliced or cubed, although it has a fairly fragile texture. There is also a smooth variety known as silken tofu, which is easy to blend into soups, sauces and drinks, giving them a creamy consistency. Smoked and ready-marinated tofu is now available. Your first taste of tofu may put you off, but persevere. It is well worth trying to introduce tofu to your diet as it is a quick-cooking food with terrific nutritional value and very useful to anyone with allergies to dairy products. Regular tofu will keep for several days in the refrigerator, but is not suitable for freezing. Silken tofu will keep for months in its pack.

My Japanese friends flavour silken tofu with spring onions, soy sauce and sesame seeds to make an accompaniment for noodles. Firm or regular tofu is excellent in a stir-fry, although I find it much too bland unless marinated in a well-flavoured mixture. Once marinated, it can also be baked or barbecued and served with a sauce. If added to a stew it will absorb the other flavours.

**Quorn** comes from a tiny mushroom-like plant which was discovered in the late 1960s. It is a pale biscuit colour and has a slightly dry, quite chewy texture and a very delicate flavour, which some think is like chicken. Being low in fat, high in protein and a good source of fibre, Quorn is an excellent addition to a vegetarian diet.

Quorn is sold as pieces and as mince. The pieces are robust and don't break up when cooked, so they can be used in both slow-cooked casseroles and stir-fries. There is no wastage or preparation – you simply take them out of the packet. The mince, which looks a little like finely chopped spaghetti, doesn't crumble when cooked in the way that meat mince does; use it to make lasagne, bolognaise sauces and pie fillings. Quorn is sold chilled and can be frozen.

Among the numerous **meat-free fast foods** are sausages and burgers made from soya protein, tofu, Quorn, nuts or lentils. There are also nuggets, cutlets and even bacon. Some products are bland, others are spicy or well flavoured with herbs – try a variety to find the ones that suit your taste. Ready-made bangers can be part of a quick children's tea, and sausages and burgers are good for barbecues. These fast foods are useful back-ups as most will keep for a few days in the refrigerator or can be cooked from frozen. From a nutritional point of view, they can be a good source of protein and fibre and may have useful amounts of vitamins and minerals, but watch out for the fat content: this varies considerably from one product to another and can be quite high.

**WINE**

It is often assumed that if a wine is a good match with fish and chicken, then it is suitable for serving with vegetarian food. Whilst there is some truth in this, I certainly don't find that a light white wine will go with all the recipes in this book. Vegetarian food has a wide spectrum of tastes: though some dishes may not be as strong as meat, they do range from subtle and mild to aromatic and spicy. So how should you go about choosing wine to go with vegetarian meals? It is an enormous subject and one that, in the end, comes down to personal preference, but here are a few points for you to consider.

First, try to match the weight of the food with a wine of a similar weight, so they work together and one doesn't overpower the other. A robust and flavourful dish works best with a full-bodied wine, while a light and delicate dish should be partnered with wine of a similar character. This applies whether the wine is red or white, although in general reds tend to have more body than whites. As a rule of thumb, wines from warmer climates, such as Australia, South Africa, California, South America and the Mediterranean area tend to have more colour, body and alcohol, in other words more weight, than wines from cooler climates, such as New Zealand, Germany, and much of France and England, although the flavours of the latter can still be intense.

Examples of full-bodied red wines include most New World Shiraz and Cabernet Sauvignon reds, southern French reds and many southern Spanish and Italian wines. For a full-bodied white, try an oak-aged Chardonnay or Semillon from the New World. Less weighty, but still substantial reds include those from Bordeaux and Burgundy, Rioja and Chianti to name a few. For medium-bodied whites try Australian Riesling, Pinot Blanc from Alsace, or Soave or Frascati from northern Italy. Light-bodied reds would include many reds from the Loire and Beaujolais regions of France, and most reds from Alsace, Germany, New Zealand and England.

Apart from matching the weight of the wine to your food, think about the flavours in the dish. Is it characterised by herbs or spices, or smoky or earthy flavours? Is it sweet or acidic? Wines can echo all of these qualities or balance them; you need to decide how to link the two. For example, you could mirror the flavour of a spicy dish with a spicy, pungent wine such as Gewürztraminer from Alsace. Similarly, you could echo the robust aromas and flavours of a tomato and herb dish with an oak-aged Shiraz from Australia or Syrah from southern France. Alternatively, you could serve a rich, creamy dish with a crisp acidic wine such as a Sauvignon Blanc from New Zealand, the acidity acting as a foil to the richness of the dish. Another example of this approach is serving a sweet wine, such as Sauternes or Vouvray, with a salty blue cheese such as Roquefort. In this case, the contrast between the food and the wine heightens the flavour of both.

Finally, remember that there are no hard and fast rules, only guidelines — and lots of pleasurable experimentation ahead. I hope these notes will encourage you to be bold in your choices, and to try some unfamiliar wines and food and wine combinations. Above all, have fun.

# SOUP

A SOUP CAN BE A NUTRITIOUS PICK-ME-UP or a great way to make a quick dish out of virtually nothing. Served with good bread and followed by something as simple as a cheese platter, with fruit or a light salad, you have a satisfying meal. And soups are easy to make – once prepared and simmering away, they demand little attention.

Most soups can be made in advance, and even benefit from reheating, which makes them useful for quick midweek meals if you are dashing home, wanting something instantly warming and comforting. They are equally good for entertaining as you can get well ahead with your preparations. Soups generally freeze well, so it's a good idea to make plenty and freeze in suitable portions.

There is a wide variety of recipes in this chapter, from the simplest of purées to more sophisticated soups containing cream and wine. There are spicy soups to bring your taste buds to life, creamy soups with a delicate flavour and hearty soups that can make a 'meal in the bowl'. Whilst I have to say that hot soups are my favourites, I love a really tasty chilled soup on a summer's day, so I have included a simple but very effective Gazpacho recipe.

## NOTES FOR YOUR STORECUPBOARD
◆

- ◆ There are many different types of vegetarian stock on the market, both in cube and powder form. Some have the distinctive taste of yeast extract, while others have an onion or mainly vegetable base. It is worth trying a range to see which you enjoy.
- ◆ The soaking water from dried wild mushrooms can be a soup base, too.
- ◆ Tinned tomatoes and passata are valuable storecupboard ingredients for making great soups.
- ◆ Silken tofu can be used in an instant non-dairy cream soup.

## TIPS FOR NO-FUSS SOUPS
◆

- ✔ most root vegetables make great soups that don't need further thickening
- ✔ pep up a bland soup with a dash of lemon or orange juice
- ✔ don't always purée the whole soup – leave half in chunks for a different texture
- ✔ a few chopped herbs, such as chives or parsley, make a lively garnish. Just snip with scissors straight over the bowl
- ✔ make easy croutons by tossing cubes of bread in seasoned oil and baking until crisp

# Spiced Dhal Soup

- ◆ gluten free
- ◆ nut free
- ◆ dairy free
- ◆ suitable for freezing

2 tablespoons sunflower oil
2 carrots, diced
1 large potato, peeled and diced
100 g/4 oz frozen peas
1 onion, chopped
¼ teaspoon chilli powder
½ teaspoon turmeric
½ teaspoon mustard powder
1 x 400 g/14 oz tin
chopped tomatoes
1 tablespoon tomato purée
50g/2 oz red lentils
1 x 1 cm/½ in piece of root
ginger, peeled and grated
3 cloves
juice of ½ lemon
1 teaspoon sugar
about 600 ml/1 pint
vegetable stock
salt
2 – 3 tablespoons chopped
fresh coriander

**HOT SPICES**
◆
If you find something a bit too
fiery, extra sugar and salt can help
reduce the temperature.

This soup, with its colourful mixture of vegetables and lentils cooked in a spiced tomato stock, is almost a meal in itself. You can keep to the spicy theme by serving it with Onion Fritters (page 45) as well as bought naan bread. Alternatively, go for a salad. This soup will freeze, but do not keep it very long because of the spices.

◆ In a large saucepan, heat the oil and gently fry the carrots, potato, peas and onion. Sprinkle over the chilli powder, turmeric and mustard and stir well. Cook the vegetables until fairly soft, stirring frequently.

◆ Add the chopped tomatoes, tomato purée, red lentils, ginger, cloves, lemon juice and sugar. Pour in the stock. Bring to the boil, then simmer for about 1 hour or until the lentils are very soft. Stir occasionally during cooking and add more stock if necessary. Season with salt.

◆ Just before serving, stir in most of the fresh coriander; use the rest to garnish each bowl.

# Cream of Cauliflower and Almond Soup with Nutmeg

The basis for this soup is a simple almond milk made with stock and ground almonds. The trick is not to use too many almonds, otherwise the finished soup will be heavy, with a coarse texture. For speed I suggest using ground almonds, although the best flavour will come if you start with unblanched whole nuts. For these you must first remove the skins by soaking the nuts in boiling water, then grind them very finely. It is a bit fiddly, but worth it for a special occasion.

◆ gluten free
◆ sugar free
◆ dairy free
◆ not suitable for freezing

25 g/1 oz ground almonds
600 ml/1 pint light vegetable stock
1 tablespoon sunflower oil
1 onion, chopped
1 leek, chopped
1 small cauliflower, divided into florets
1 bay leaf
grated nutmeg
salt and pepper

◆ Whizz the ground almonds with the stock in a blender or food processor. The resulting liquid should have the consistency of thin milk.

◆ In a large saucepan, heat the oil and gently fry the onion and leek until soft. Then add the cauliflower florets and cook gently for 5–6 minutes. Pour over the almond stock and add the bay leaf and a generous grating of nutmeg. Bring the mixture to the boil, then simmer for 15 minutes or until the cauliflower is very soft. Leave to cool slightly. Purée the soup and season well. Reheat gently before serving.

# Butternut and Carrot Soup with Ginger

♦ gluten free
♦ sugar free
♦ nut free
♦ dairy free
♦ suitable for freezing

2 tablespoons sunflower oil
1 onion, chopped
1 clove garlic, crushed
1 teaspoon freshly grated
root ginger
700 g/1½ lb butternut squash,
seeds and fibres removed (not
peeled), then chopped
250 g/8 oz carrots, chopped
600–900 ml/1–1½ pints
vegetable stock
2 teaspoons fresh thyme
1 bay leaf
grated zest and juice of 1 lemon
salt and pepper

With its warm orange colour and delicate nutty flavour, butternut squash is a versatile vegetable, useful in casseroles, roasted vegetable combinations and, especially, soup. It has similarities with root vegetables such as carrots and parsnips in that, once cooked, it will purée to a very smooth, creamy consistency. I've added some carrots to enhance the colour and ginger for a warm flavour. For a special occasion garnish each serving with a dollop of cream or soured cream.

♦ In a large saucepan, heat the oil and gently cook the onion and garlic. Add the ginger, butternut squash and carrots and cook gently, covered, for 10 minutes. Add the stock, thyme and bay leaf . Bring to the boil, then cover the pan again and simmer for 40 minutes or until the vegetables are really tender. Cool slightly, then remove the bay leaf and whizz the soup in a blender or food processor until smooth. Season to taste with lemon zest and juice, salt and pepper. Reheat before serving.

### BUTTERNUT SQUASH
♦

Although the outer skin looks indigestible, it does become tender during cooking and will purée to a smooth texture. By not peeling the squash you'll save time and this will also increase the flavour of the finished soup. Squash will keep for several months in the right conditions – cool, dry and dark.

# Deep Green Watercress Soup

This is a marvellous soup, with good colour and a smooth texture, and it's packed full of vitamins. I often make it in the colder months as it seems to give me a real boost as well as warding off winter chills. Serve it as a light snack on its own, or as a starter before a more substantial dish such as Spicy Chick Peas with Couscous (page 112) or Stuffed Field Mushrooms with Mozzarella (page 73). For a richer version, add some crème fraîche.

◆ Heat the oil in a saucepan and cook the onion gently for about 5 minutes. Add the potato and watercress and sweat the vegetables, covered, for about 3 minutes. Pour on the stock and bring to the boil. Cover the pan again and simmer for about 20 minutes or until the potatoes are very soft.

◆ Allow the soup to cool for a few minutes, then whizz in a food processor or blender until smooth. Season to taste.

◆ Return the soup to the pan and heat through before serving.

*Illustrated overleaf*

◆ sugar free
◆ nut free
◆ dairy free
◆ suitable for freezing

2 tablespoons olive oil
1 onion, finely chopped
1 small potato, peeled
and chopped
2 or 3 packets of
watercress, washed
600 ml/1 pint vegetable stock
salt and pepper

### WATERCRESS
◆

Iron is a vital mineral in the vegetarian diet, and it is more readily absorbed by the body if eaten along with a food containing vitamin C. Watercress is a good source of both iron and vitamin C, so try to use it frequently. Apart from soup it can be used in salads and sandwiches or chopped finely into a sauce or mayonnaise.

# Red Pepper, Tomato and Tofu Soup

♦ gluten free

♦ sugar free

♦ nut free

♦ dairy free

♦ not suitable for freezing

2 medium-sized red peppers
2 tablespoons olive oil
1 onion, finely chopped
1 clove garlic, crushed
1 teaspoon dried marjoram
1 teaspoon dried thyme
1 x 400 g/14 oz tin chopped
tomatoes
2 tablespoons tomato purée
300 ml/ ½ pint vegetable stock
½ teaspoon paprika
300 g/10 oz silken tofu
salt and pepper

This is a nourishing light soup, ideal for a summer lunch or supper. Roasted peppers and Mediterranean herbs give the soup a good flavour, while the silken tofu provides a creamy finish.

◆ Lightly oil the peppers and pierce once or twice. Roast in the oven preheated to 200°C/400°F/gas 6 for 30 minutes or until well charred on all sides. Cool, then peel off the skin and remove the seeds. Chop the flesh roughly.

◆ In a large saucepan, heat the rest of the oil and gently fry the onion and garlic until soft. Add the chopped red peppers, herbs, tinned tomatoes, tomato purée, stock and paprika. Bring the mixture to the boil, then cover and simmer for 30 minutes. Leave to cool slightly.

◆ Whizz the silken tofu in a blender or food processor until smooth. Add the tomato and pepper mixture and whizz until smooth and creamy. Season well, and heat through gently before serving.

*Illustrated on pages 138 – 139, with Corn Bread (page 137)*

# Wild Mushroom Soup with Cream and Wine

This is a rich soup made in two stages, both of which can be done well ahead of time for easy entertaining. Wild mushrooms have an intense woody aroma that is almost overpowering if you smell them in the packet, but in the soup, the flavour of the mushrooms is delicate and subtle. Follow this with a rice dish, such as Cashew and Saffron Pilaff (page 104) or Cajun Quorn and Rice with White Wine (page 108), or with a pastry, for example Gougère with Leeks and White Wine (page 118) or Chestnut Pie with Herbs (page 115).

♦ sugar free
♦ nut free
♦ suitable for freezing

25 g/1 oz dried wild mushrooms preferably cep or porcini
300 ml/½ pint boiling water
50 g/2 oz butter
2 large onions, finely chopped
250 g/8 oz fresh chestnut mushrooms, finely sliced
2 cloves garlic, crushed
50 ml/2 fl oz white wine
2 tablespoons finely chopped fresh parsley
1 tablespoon flour
300 ml/½ pint milk
salt and pepper

◆ Rinse the dried mushrooms, pour the boiling water over them and soak for half an hour. In a large saucepan, melt half of the butter and cook the onions for 5–7 minutes or until soft but not coloured. Add the sliced chestnut mushrooms and the crushed garlic and cook for a further 5 minutes.

◆ Drain the soaked dried mushrooms, reserving the liquid. Add the dried mushrooms to the onion and mushroom mixture and cook for 2–3 minutes, stirring. Add the white wine, bring to the boil and simmer for 3 minutes, then add the soaking liquid and parsley. Bring back to the boil, cover and simmer for 30 minutes.

◆ Melt the remaining butter in a small saucepan. Add the flour and stir in to make a roux. Add the milk and bring to the boil, stirring frequently, to make a smooth white sauce. Leave to cool slightly.

◆ Whizz the two mixtures together using a food processor or blender. Season well, and heat through before serving.

# Gazpacho

♦ gluten free
♦ sugar free
♦ nut free
♦ dairy free
♦ not suitable for freezing

1 small cucumber, peeled
and cubed
6 tomatoes, peeled and diced
1 small red onion, finely diced
1 clove garlic, crushed
1 tablespoon red wine vinegar
1 tablespoon olive oil
2 tablespoons chopped
fresh parsley
450 ml/¾ pint tomato juice
½ teaspoon ground cinnamon
1 bay leaf
6 cloves
salt and pepper

This is a classic summer soup and one of my favourites, not least because it is extremely easy to make. Two golden rules for success are: make it well ahead of time so that the flavours can develop, and serve it well chilled (if you need to cheat you can always add a little crushed ice as a garnish). Serve gazpacho with good cheese, bread and a selection of fruits for a light summer lunch. For a more substantial meal, follow it with Stilton and Courgette Strudel (page 116) or Spinach and Feta Quiche (page 114) plus salads and new potatoes.

♦ Combine the vegetables in a large bowl. Add the remaining ingredients and mix carefully but thoroughly. Leave for at least 2 hours to allow the flavours to blend. Before serving remove the bay leaf and cloves.

# STARTERS AND SIDE SALADS

TRADITIONALLY, SERVING A STARTER suggested that there would be, perhaps, two or three more courses to follow. But nowadays a starter can easily be the main focus of a meal, particularly if you are just looking for something light and tempting or preparing food for one or two. In addition, several starters can be combined together to make an interesting and more substantial meal.

The starters in this chapter range from robust ones with powerful flavours to those that are more delicate or light and fruity. They are all cold, so they work just as well as side dishes. If you are serving them in this way, remember to choose combinations that will provide contrasts in taste, texture and colour.

Also in this chapter are some notes about salad leaves and one or two ideas for simple but effective dressings. A green salad is surely the easiest way to put instant colour on the table, and these days the choice of leaves is marvellously wide, enabling you to serve a different combination virtually every day. I make the most of the prepared bagged mixtures to save time and wastage.

### NOTES FOR YOUR STORECUPBOARD
◆

◆ Many of these starters rely on a well-flavoured dressing, so you should have on hand a good-quality olive oil and a wine or cider vinegar.
◆ Tahini, a sesame seed paste (similar to peanut butter), is very useful for dips and dressings. It mixes well with numerous flavourings such as oil, lemon juice, yoghurt or soy sauce and is an excellent source of calcium.

### TIPS FOR NO-FUSS STARTERS AND SIDE SALADS
◆

✔ if you have only one leafy salad ingredient, add extra bits and pieces to it such as chopped nuts or roasted seeds, sliced apple, olives or crumbled cheese
✔ lightweight salads are best tossed at the last minute in oil-based dressings
✔ when serving heavyweight dressings, spoon them over the top or serve separately as a dip
✔ boost a salad into a main course by serving it with a couscous dish (see page 140) or pasta
✔ children seem to find separate salad ingredients more appealing than a mixture, and it only takes seconds to arrange pieces on their plates in an attractive pattern

# Roast Aubergines with Garlic, Sesame Dressing and Lebanese Tabbouleh

♦ sugar free
♦ not suitable for freezing

2 aubergines
2 tablespoons olive oil
salt and pepper

*For the dressing*
4–6 cloves garlic
2 tablespoons tahini
4 tablespoons water
2 tablespoons lemon juice
4 tablespoons plain yoghurt

*For the tabbouleh*
50 g/2 oz bulgar wheat
¼ teaspoon salt
100 ml/3½ fl oz boiling water
1 tablespoon lemon juice
1 tablespoon olive oil
9–10 tablespoons finely chopped
mixed fresh coriander and parsley

---

**ROASTING GARLIC**
♦
When roasting garlic, the cloves do not need to be peeled. You may think that 4–6 cloves is a lot, but don't worry because roasted garlic is quite different from raw, being sweeter and more subtle in flavour.

---

Succulent roast aubergine slices on a deep green herb tabbouleh topped with a subtle dressing makes a lovely combination of colours and flavours. This can be served as a starter followed by a casserole or pastry dish, or increase the quantities and serve it as a light salad meal accompanied by a tomato salad or roast vegetables.

♦ Slice the aubergines thickly and brush the slices with seasoned olive oil. Roast in the oven preheated to 200°C/400°F/gas 6 for 15–20 minutes. Leave to cool.

♦ Roast the garlic cloves in the oven for 5 minutes. Cool slightly, then peel and mash well. Mix the tahini with the water. Add the mashed roasted garlic, lemon juice and yoghurt.

♦ For the tabbouleh, put the bulgar wheat and salt into a large bowl, pour over the boiling water and leave to stand for 30 minutes. The water should all be absorbed, but if necessary drain the bulgar wheat. Add the lemon juice and olive oil and mix in the chopped herbs. Season to taste.

♦ Arrange the tabbouleh on individual plates or a large platter, top with the aubergine slices and spoon over the dressing. Serve at room temperature.

# Artichoke and Goat's Cheese Pâté with Roast Peppers and Courgettes

This is a great recipe, just a simple combination of a few ingredients but one that is very effective. You can serve the pâté on its own, but I like the colourful addition of the roast vegetables. Roasting vegetables brings out their sweetness, which is complemented by aromatic balsamic vinegar. I suggest following this starter with a pasta or rice dish. Or make it into a *mezze* meal by adding extra roast vegetables and serving some of the *tapas* ideas on pages 47 – 49.

◆ To make the pâté, cream the goat's cheese with the butter until smooth. Finely chop the walnuts and artichoke hearts by hand so that the pieces are fairly even, then stir them into the mixture. Season well. If prepared ahead of time, keep the pâté in the fridge, but allow to return to room temperature before serving.

◆ Cut the peppers into thick strips and the courgettes into long strips and toss in the seasoned olive oil. Place on a baking tray and roast in the oven preheated to 200°C/400°F/gas 6 for 20–25 minutes or until the pieces look well roasted. Scrape all the pieces and oily residue into a large bowl, add the balsamic vinegar and toss together. Leave to cool.

◆ Arrange the pâté on individual plates with a portion of roast vegetables, or on a large platter. Serve with savoury crackers.

♦ gluten free (without the crackers)
♦ sugar free
♦ not suitable for freezing

*For the pâté*
150 g/5 oz soft goat's cheese
50 g/2 oz butter
50 g/2 oz walnut pieces
4 tinned artichoke hearts
salt and pepper

*For the roast vegetables*
2 red peppers
2 courgettes
2–3 tablespoons olive oil
1–2 tablespoons balsamic vinegar

*To serve*
savoury crackers or water biscuits

# Asparagus with Lemon and Roasted Hazelnuts

♦ sugar free

♦ dairy free

♦ not suitable for freezing

2 bunches of asparagus

*For the dressing*
75 g / 3 oz hazelnuts
2 tablespoons mixed chopped fresh parsley and tarragon
2 tablespoons lemon juice
1 clove garlic
salt and pepper
150 ml / ¼ pint mixed hazelnut oil and olive oil
1 teaspoon grated lemon zest

Asparagus makes an easy and elegant starter, and hazelnuts are a good partner. For an even simpler version, just serve the asparagus with melted butter and garnish with roasted hazelnuts.

♦ First make the dressing. Toast the hazelnuts in the oven preheated to 190°C/375°F/gas 5 for 5–6 minutes. Cool, then rub off the skins using your hands or by wrapping in a cloth. Roughly chop 25 g/1 oz of the hazelnuts and set aside. Finely grind the remaining nuts in a blender or food processor. Add the herbs and blend thoroughly for a few seconds. Add the lemon juice, garlic and seasoning. Blend again, then gradually add the oil with the machine running. Finally, stir in the lemon zest and adjust the seasoning.

♦ Prepare the asparagus by trimming off the woody stem ends. Place in a tall saucepan of boiling water, with the stems in the water and the tips above so that they steam. Cook for 8–10 minutes. Drain well and leave to cool. Arrange each portion on individual plates and pour some of the dressing over. Garnish with the chopped roasted hazelnuts.

### NUT OILS
♦
Dressings made with nuts and nut oils are rich in flavour. For the best results, use either walnuts or hazelnuts and the corresponding oils. Mix the nut oil with some olive oil or good-quality sunflower oil. Vary the proportions according to taste. These dressings work well with steamed or roasted vegetables as well as chunky salads.

*Illustrated on pages 34 – 35 (right)*

# Avocado with Smoked Tofu and Arame

I love avocado combined with sharp citrus flavours and soy sauce. This mixture goes well with smoked tofu and the delicate seaweed called arame, making a starter with an Oriental theme. Sorrel or rocket leaves can be added to give additional tang.

◆ Soak the arame in hot water for 15 minutes, then drain well. Lightly toast the sesame seeds in a dry frying pan.

◆ To make the dressing, mix the lime zest and juice with the sesame oil and shoyu. Stir in the arame and the spring onions. Season to taste. Chop or slice the avocados and tofu and toss gently in the dressing.

◆ To serve, arrange the salad leaves on a large platter and top with the avocado and tofu plus any remaining dressing. Garnish with the sesame seeds.

◆ sugar free
◆ dairy free
◆ not suitable for freezing

25 g/1 oz dried arame
1 tablespoon sesame seeds
2 spring onions, cut into fine strips
2 avocados
125 g/4 oz smoked tofu
200 g/7 oz salad leaves, such as lamb's lettuce, baby spinach and watercress

*For the dressing*
grated zest and juice of 1 lime
1 tablespoon sesame oil
1 tablespoon soy sauce
salt and pepper.

**SOY SAUCE**

There are now many varieties of this tasty sauce on sale in both supermarkets and health food shops. Some do contain artificial colouring and additives. Look out for shoyu, which is usually just fermented soya beans, wheat and salt. For those on a wheat-free diet, check on tamari, another fermented soy product that may not contain wheat.

# Italian Tomato Salad with Balsamic Vinegar

♦ gluten free
♦ nut free
♦ dairy free
♦ not suitable for freezing

2 or 3 beef tomatoes, sliced
½ teaspoon salt
½ teaspoon sugar
freshly ground black pepper
1 teaspoon balsamic vinegar

Balsamic vinegar is ideal with slightly sweet ingredients – hence the unusual sounding but now classic strawberries and balsamic vinegar combination. I also find it complements tomatoes very well. This well-seasoned tomato salad is so useful as it is simple, colourful and tasty. With this salad and a simple green leaf mixture, you've immediately got a colourful background to enhance any meal. Serve this with some of the pastry recipes on pages 114–118 or with several of the Express Eating ideas on pages 63–74. Or add a few slices of mozzarella to make a super sandwich filling.

◆ Arrange the tomato slices in a single layer on a large plate. Mix together the salt and sugar and add plenty of freshly ground black pepper. Sprinkle this mixture over the tomato slices, then sprinkle over the balsamic vinegar.

◆ Leave the tomatoes at room temperature for half an hour before serving.

# Cashew and Mango Salad with Citrus Dressing

This is a most refreshing savoury fruit salad. Serve it as a starter before a substantial main course, such as a pastry dish or casserole. It also works well as a side salad.

- ◆ gluten free
- ◆ sugar free
- ◆ dairy free
- ◆ not suitable for freezing

50 g/2 oz cashew nuts
1 tablespoon sesame seeds
1 large orange
50 ml/2 fl oz sunflower oil
salt and pepper
1 mango
1 Romaine or Cos lettuce

◆ Roast the cashew nuts in the oven preheated to 200°C/400°F/gas 6 for 5 minutes or until golden brown. Leave to cool, then chop very roughly. Toast the sesame seeds in a dry frying pan for 1 minute.

◆ Zest the orange, then cut in half. Squeeze the juice from one half and mix with the oil. Add the orange zest. Season lightly. Peel and segment the remaining half. Put the segments in a bowl. Peel the mango, cut round the stone and then cut the flesh into small pieces. Mix with the orange segments and add the toasted cashew nuts. Pour the orange juice and oil dressing over the fruit and nut mixture.

◆ Line a bowl with lettuce leaves, pile in the fruit salad and garnish with the toasted sesame seeds.

*Illustrated overleaf (left)*

# Salad Leaves

♦ gluten free

♦ sugar free

♦ nut free

♦ dairy free

♦ suitable for freezing

A leaf salad is an easy accompaniment, a simple way of brightening a meal or creating a contrast, and if fresh it is a good source of nutrients, particularly vitamins. You'll see that I often suggest a leaf salad, but in each case I would put together a slightly different combination to complement the main dish.

To help you with mixing leaves, here are some of the best known, which I have divided into colour groups:

**Pale green**

Chicory: clean, slightly bitter taste and crisp texture

Chinese leaves: delicate flavour with softer outer leaves

Iceberg: crisp texture but little flavour

**Soft or mid green**

Lamb's lettuce: succulent and mild in flavour

Butterhead or round lettuce: soft leaves with a mild flavour

Rocket: attractive notched leaves with a peppery flavour

**Bright green**

Cos and Romaine lettuce: large leaves, crisp and refreshing

Endive or frisée: curly, jagged leaves with a slight bitterness

Little Gem: crisp and sweet with small leaves

Sorrel: slender leaves with a peppery lemon tang

**Dark green**

Spinach: small, soft leaves with a sharp taste

Watercress: strong, assertive flavour

**Red or purple**

Lollo Rosso (also green); frilled leaves with a delicate flavour

Oakleaf lettuce: attractive maroon edge and dark interior

Radicchio: strongly flavoured, crunchy leaves ribbed with white.

### SALAD LEAVES
♦

When buying salad ingredients, reject anything that looks wilted or bruised. Remove tight polythene packaging as soon as possible and keep the leaves in the refrigerator. Ready-mixed salad ingredients are packed in special bags to keep them fresh. In this case keep the salad leaves in the bag, but once you have opened the packet use the leaves as soon as possible.

# Classic Vinaigrette

This should strictly be called *my* classic vinaigrette, because although based on the French version I prefer a whole grain mustard to a smooth French mustard for flavouring and a concentrated apple juice for sweetening rather than sugar. I usually make a large quantity and then keep it in a screw-top bottle, ready to dress salad leaves.

◆ Mix the olive oil with the vinegar. Then add the remaining ingredients and shake together well. Adjust the sweetening, flavouring and seasoning according to taste. Store in a bottle at a cool temperature.

◆ sugar free
◆ nut free
◆ dairy free
◆ not suitable for freezing

150 ml/¼ pint good-quality olive oil
2 tablespoons white wine or cider vinegar
1 clove garlic, crushed with salt
½–1 teaspoon whole grain mustard
1–2 teaspoons concentrated apple juice
pepper

**FLAVOURING IDEAS**
◆
There are plenty of ways to vary this recipe. Add a couple of tablespoons of chopped fresh herbs, such as chives or tarragon, or replace some of the olive oil with a flavoured oil such as chilli oil or walnut oil.

# Tahini Dressing

♦ sugar free
♦ dairy free
♦ not suitable for freezing

2–3 tablespoons tahini
3–4 tablespoons water
juice of ½ lemon
2 tablespoons olive oil
1–2 tablespoons soy sauce

This well-flavoured dressing works well with robust salad ingredients such as raw carrot, celery and pepper. It is also wonderful on roast vegetable mixtures, and can be used to boost a stir-fry. You can alter the consistency of the dressing by adding more water or lemon juice; more oil will tend to thicken it. A favourite variation of mine is to stir in some plain yoghurt.

♦ Mix the tahini with the water in a small bowl. Add more water if the mixture looks too dry. Then add the lemon juice, oil and soy sauce to taste. Stir very well to blend.

# Tofu Mayonnaise

♦ gluten free
♦ sugar free
♦ nut free
♦ not suitable for freezing

1 packet silken tofu
juice of 1 lemon
1–2 cloves garlic, crushed
6 tablespoons olive oil
salt and pepper

Silken tofu is the basis of a very easy, creamy dairy-free dressing. Use this as a substitute for egg-based mayonnaise.

♦ Using a food processor or blender, blend the tofu with the lemon juice and garlic. Then add the oil and blend thoroughly. Season to taste. Use as required.

# SNACKS, SMALL SAVOURIES AND SANDWICHES

MY LOVE OF COOKING INITIALLY SPRANG FROM THE PLEASURE to be had from sitting down and sharing food with friends. Whilst I still do this occasionally, more often than not meals have to be speedy affairs, squeezed in between one thing and another. This is when small snacks, finger foods and light meals come into their own, to give a quick energy boost.

The ideas in this chapter – which I like to think is subtitled 'food on the go' – work in several ways. They can be served as savoury snacks, or used in packed lunches, or handed round as pre-prandial nibbles before a more formal meal. When eaten in quantity these snacks can make quite a meal, especially if you serve two or three dishes together plus a side salad or two. I think this a very good, casual way of entertaining, much less effort to prepare than a three-course menu.

Many countries have marvellous ideas for savouries with a difference. I have included some spicy Indian onion fritters as well as Italian toasts and tapas from Spain. There are some snacks here that will particularly appeal to children. My sons especially enjoy filo parcels as well as the cheese 'sausages' which we still call bangers.

---

**NOTES FOR YOUR STORECUPBOARD**
◆

◆ Keep on hand some gram flour, which is the basis for Indian fritters.
◆ Jars of olives are a good standby. Try both plain and herbed varieties.
◆ It is useful to have some filo pastry in the freezer. As it is sold in large packets I prefer to buy it fresh and then rewrap in useful numbers of sheets so that I don't have to thaw the whole lot.

---

**TIPS FOR NO-FUSS SNACKS AND SANDWICHES**
◆

✔ ring the changes with sandwiches by using different breads or rolls
✔ a bought olive paste or whole grain mustard can perk up a plain sandwich
✔ plain yoghurt makes a good dipping sauce, especially if flavoured with a little toasted cumin
✔ snacks can be quite high in fat, so compensate by also eating lots of plain salads

# Parmesan Profiteroles

♦ sugar free
♦ some filling suggestions are nut free
♦ not suitable for freezing

150 ml/¼ pint water
50 g/2 oz butter
60 g/2½ oz plain white flour
2 eggs, beaten
25 g/1 oz Parmesan cheese,
freshly grated

Choux pastry is not at all hard to make. The most important point is to have everything measured before you start. Then work quickly and beat the mixture very well. The buns should be baked until crisp, otherwise they may collapse. If you don't think they are done in the time I have suggested, turn your oven down a little and give them another 5–10 minutes.

◆ Bring the water and butter to the boil. When the butter has melted and the liquid is boiling, shoot in all the flour. Beat well, removing from the heat. Add one egg and beat in until completely absorbed. Then add the other egg. Mix in the Parmesan, reserving a little for dusting.

◆ Spoon walnut-sized blobs of the mixture on to a greased baking sheet. Sprinkle over the remaining grated Parmesan. Bake in the oven preheated to 200°C/400°F/gas 6 for 20 minutes. Cool on a wire rack. When cold, split and fill.

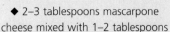

SUGGESTIONS FOR FILLINGS
◆

◆ 2–3 tablespoons mascarpone cheese mixed with 1–2 tablespoons pesto sauce

◆ 2–3 tablespoons cream cheese mixed with chopped fresh herbs, such as chives and basil, or with spices such as paprika or cayenne

◆ Roquefort cheese mashed and mixed with toasted chopped walnuts

# Olive and Pepper Strudels

These tasty pastries make ideal picnic or packed lunch fare as well as looking great on a buffet table or for a light lunch. Once the pepper is roasted the filling is very easy to make using a food processor or blender. I think filo is best eaten on the day it is made, but at a pinch these would last to a second day if kept in the fridge.

♦ sugar free
♦ dairy free
♦ not suitable for freezing

12 sheets of filo pastry
50–75 ml/2–3 fl oz olive oil

*For the filling*
1 red pepper
2 tablespoons olive oil
1 onion, finely chopped
2 cloves garlic, crushed
8 sun-dried tomatoes
(packed in oil)
125 g/4 oz pitted black olives
4 tablespoons chopped fresh basil
25 g/1 oz pine kernels
salt and pepper

◆ Brush the red pepper with a little oil and pierce the skin. Roast in the oven preheated to 200°C/400°F/gas 6 for 30 minutes or until the skin is charred all over. Leave to cool, then peel off the skin and remove the seeds. Chop the flesh roughly.

◆ Heat the rest of the oil and gently fry the onion and garlic until soft. Cool slightly, then scrape them with any oil into a food processor or blender. Add the red pepper, tomatoes, olives, basil and pine kernels. Process until fairly smooth. Season to taste. Divide into 12 portions.

◆ Lay one sheet of filo pastry on the work surface and brush well with olive oil. Spoon a portion of filling in a line along the middle third of the sheet, leaving the side thirds clear and a small margin at the top. Fold over the margin to cover the filling, then fold in the sides. Roll up to make a cigar shape. Brush well with more oil and place on a baking tray. Repeat with the remaining sheets of pastry and filling. Bake the strudels in the oven preheated to 200°C/400°F/gas 6 for 20 minutes or until crisp. Serve warm or at room temperature.

*Illustrated overleaf*

# Cheese and Herb Savouries

♦ sugar free
♦ nut free
♦ suitable for freezing

175 g/6 oz wholemeal
breadcrumbs
125 g/4 oz mature Cheddar
cheese, grated
2 tablespoons finely chopped
fresh parsley
3 spring onions, finely chopped
1 tablespoon soya flour
1 teaspoon whole grain mustard
1 egg, beaten
1 egg, separated
salt and pepper
oil for frying

There are many vegetarian sausages available now, generally made from tofu or soya protein, but I still enjoy this classic recipe. It is useful for party snacks, picnics and children's suppers or lunch boxes. A well-flavoured cheese is essential as is generous seasoning. Freeze uncooked.

♦ Set aside 50 g/2 oz of the breadcrumbs. Mix the remaining crumbs with the cheese, parsley, spring onions, soya flour and mustard. Add the beaten whole egg and egg yolk and season well. Divide the mixture into 8–12 pieces and shape each into a small sausage. Lightly beat the egg white. Roll each sausage in egg white and then in the reserved breadcrumbs. Shallow fry in hot oil for 5–7 minutes, turning several times to colour and cook evenly. Drain on kitchen paper.

### SOYA FLOUR
♦

Soya flour is unlike other flours in that it has a high fat content. Treat it as an enriching ingredient and add a tablespoonful or two to a standard cake or pastry mixture. Soya flour is a useful source of B vitamins, iron and calcium.

# Onion Fritters with Fresh Coriander Dip

These make a great snack or starter, and are best eaten on the day they are made. It is less messy to chop the onion, but I don't think the end result is such fun because the onion rings make wonderfully weird shapes. A cool yoghurt dip is a delightful contrast. Ready-made chutneys and relishes work well too, to save time. These fritters can also be made with cauliflower florets.

◆ To make the dip, put the coriander and chilli in a blender with a little water and blend until smooth. Stir into the yoghurt and add salt and lemon juice to taste.

◆ Mix the gram flour with the garam masala, chilli powder and salt. Rub in the vegetable oil, then pour on the warm water and mix to make a smooth batter. It is best to do this with a whisk or a wooden spoon. Stir in the onion.

◆ Heat vegetable oil in a deep saucepan. Fry tablespoons of the batter, cooking about 4 fritters at a time, until they are golden brown on both sides. Drain on kitchen paper. Serve with the coriander dip.

♦ glutenfree
♦ sugar free
♦ nut free
♦ dairy free (except dip)
♦ not suitable for freezing

*For the dip*
50 g/2 oz fresh coriander,
roughly chopped
1 small fresh green chilli,
de-seeded
150 ml/¼ pint plain yoghurt
salt
lemon juice

*For the fritters*
125 g/4 oz gram flour
(chick pea flour)
1 teaspoon garam masala
¼ teaspoon chilli powder
1 teaspoon salt
2 teaspoons vegetable oil, plus
more for deep frying
150 ml/¼ pint warm water
1 onion, sliced in rings

# Bruschetta

♦ sugar free
♦ nut free
♦ not suitable for freezing

1 ciabatta loaf, cut in slices
1–2 cloves garlic, halved
olive oil
freshly grated Parmesan cheese

Bruschetta are toasted slices of ciabatta or focaccia topped with a variety of flavourings. They make very simple snacks and great nibbles prior to a party meal. You can obviously vary the toppings to fit in with whatever else you are serving.

♦ Bake the slices of bread in the oven preheated to 200°C/400°F/gas 6 for 5–7 minutes. Rub the surfaces with garlic and then brush with olive oil. Sprinkle with a little cheese and bake again briefly.

**Two bruschetta toppings**

♦ **Roast Red Pepper and Olive:** Roast and peel 2 red peppers (see page 41). Chop the flesh finely and mix with 125 g/4 oz pitted black olives, chopped, 2 tablespoons sun-dried tomato paste, 2 teaspoons capers and 2 teaspoons chopped fresh oregano. Season to taste with salt and pepper. Bake the bread as above, rub with garlic and brush with oil. Smear a little of the red pepper paste on each slice, then sprinkle on a little Parmesan. Bake again briefly and serve hot.

♦ **Onion and Caper with Feta Cheese:** Make up the onion topping on page 121 and keep it warm. Bake the bread as above, rub with garlic and brush with oil. Top with the warm onion mixture and sprinkle over the capers and 50–75 g/2–3 oz crumbled feta cheese. Serve immediately.

# Potato Wedges Baked with Herbs

A delicious starter or side dish, this could be served with Marinated Olives (page 48), Hot Mushrooms with Goat's Cheese (page 65) and Olive and Pepper Strudels (page 41) to make up a colourful buffet spread.

◆ nut free
◆ dairy free
◆ not suitable for freezing

3 cloves garlic, finely chopped
$\frac{1}{2}$ teaspoon salt
2 tablespoons olive oil
750 g/1½ lb potatoes, peeled and cut into wedges
150 ml/¼ pint Easy Tomato Sauce (page 98)
1 teaspoon chopped fresh rosemary
1 tablespoon chopped fresh oregano
2 tablespoons chopped fresh parsley
salt and pepper

◆ Crush the garlic with the salt. Heat the oil in a flameproof casserole and fry the potato pieces with the crushed garlic gently for 10 minutes or until just becoming coloured.

◆ Pour on the tomato sauce and stir in the herbs. Season well. Bring to the boil, then cover the casserole and bake in the oven preheated to 190°C/375°F/gas 5 for 40–45 minutes or until the potatoes are tender. Serve hot or warm.

# Marinated Olives

♦ gluten free
♦ sugar free
♦ nut free
♦ dairy free
♦ not suitable for freezing

black olives
6 cloves garlic, cut in pieces
4 bay leaves
24 capers
2 teaspoons dried oregano
2 teaspoons dried marjoram
olive oil

There are plenty of gourmet marinated olives to be bought in good delicatessens and supermarkets, but it is fun – and so easy – to make your own. They can double up as great gifts too.

◆ Have enough olives to fill a standard jam jar.

◆ Pack a layer of olives in the bottom of the jar and then put in a clove of garlic, a bay leaf and a scattering of capers and herbs. Repeat the layering of ingredients until the jar is full, then pour in enough olive oil to fill the jar completely. Leave at room temperature for 4–5 days before serving.

# Sauté Mushrooms with Sherry Vinegar

These can be served as tapas, or little appetisers, before dishes such as Mediterranean Frittata (page 64) or Potato Gratin Agenaise (page 74). Served hot, they also work well as an accompaniment to couscous or pastry dishes.

◆ Heat the oil in a frying pan. When hot, add the mushrooms and cook on a high heat until they are beginning to soften and exude their juices. Add the garlic, herbs and sherry vinegar. Continue cooking, stirring frequently, until the mushrooms are tender. Season well, and serve hot or at room temperature.

◆ gluten free
◆ nut free
◆ dairy free
◆ not suitable for freezing

2 tablespoons olive oil
450 g/1 lb button mushrooms, halved
1 clove garlic, crushed
3 tablespoons finely chopped fresh parsley
1 teaspoon dried marjoram
1 tablespoon sherry vinegar
salt and pepper

### A QUICK SAUCE
◆
When you need a sauce for a dish but haven't time to make one, try serving these mushrooms instead. Their succulent texture makes a good moist accompaniment.

# Yellow Pepper and Caper Spread

- ♦ gluten free
- ♦ sugar free
- ♦ nut free
- ♦ dairy free
- ♦ not suitable for freezing

2 yellow peppers
2 tablespoons capers
2 tablespoons lemon juice
2 tablespoons olive oil
1–2 cloves garlic, peeled
snipped fresh chives
salt and pepper

This is a colourful filling with the capers contrasting well with the sweet yellow pepper. It can also be used as a dip or spread.

♦ Roast the peppers whole in the oven preheated to 200°C/400°F/gas 6 for 40 minutes or until the skin is well charred all over. Leave to cool, then remove the skin and seeds.

♦ Put the pepper flesh in a blender or food processor with the remaining ingredients except the chives. Purée until smooth. Add a generous amount of finely snipped chives and season to taste.

# Aubergine and Coriander Spread

This sandwich filling is very easy to prepare. Try to make it in advance so that the flavours have a chance to blend. When assembling sandwiches, spread the mixture thickly and add Cos lettuce leaves, halved black olives and thin slices of pepper or red onion.

◆ gluten free
◆ sugar free
◆ not suitable for freezing

large aubergine
4 tablespoons crème fraîche
or thick plain yoghurt (Greek
or strained)
1–2 tablespoons lemon juice
3 tablespoons tahini
4 tablespoons finely chopped
fresh coriander
2 cloves garlic, crushed
salt and pepper

◆ Prick the skin of the aubergine and bake in the oven preheated to 180°C/350°F/gas 4 for 20–25 minutes or until soft. Remove the skin and chop the flesh.

◆ Put the aubergine flesh into a food processor or blender and add the crème fraîche or yoghurt, lemon juice, tahini, coriander and garlic. Process until smooth. Season to taste.

# Pumpkin Seed and Avocado Spread

- ◆ gluten free
- ◆ sugar free
- ◆ dairy free
- ◆ not suitable for freezing

75 g/3 oz pumpkin seeds
2–3 tablespoons olive oil
1 teaspoon cumin seeds
salt
1 clove garlic, peeled
2 tablespoons chopped
fresh coriander
a small piece of fresh green chilli
(or pinch of chilli powder)
juice of 1 lime
1 ripe avocado

Pumpkin seeds, as well as being delicious, are a good source of zinc. Here I've mixed them with creamy avocado flesh to make a well-flavoured spread which could also be used as a dip with crackers and raw vegetables.

◆ Fry the pumpkin seeds in 2 teaspoons olive oil until they begin to brown and pop. Add the cumin seeds and a little salt and continue to fry for 1–2 minutes, stirring. Leave to cool.

◆ Grind the seeds finely in a food processor or blender. Add the garlic, coriander, chilli and lime juice and blend again. Add the avocado and 1 tablespoon olive oil and blend until creamy. If necessary, add more olive oil, then adjust the seasoning.

# SIGNIFICANT SALADS

SALADS TODAY ARE SO IMAGINATIVE AND COLOURFUL, thanks in part to the inspiration of vegetarian cuisine. They are a far cry from the old days of tired leaves of lettuce and tasteless tomatoes served with cottage cheese or slices of Cheddar.

There are all manner of ingredients, both cooked and raw, that can make a salad into a satisfying meal rather than just an afterthought on the side. Additions such as rice, bulgar wheat, lentils and tofu add substance as well as nutritional value, and they are easy to prepare. There are also numerous vegetables and fruit that can be included, raw or cooked, so you can make interesting combinations of colour, taste and texture. Dressings can be varied, too, using ingredients such as soft cheeses and sun-dried tomatoes, and flavourings of fresh herbs or exotic spices.

The salads featured in this chapter are 'significant' not just because they are filling but also because they provide a good nutritional combination, with plenty of carbohydrate and protein as well as vital vitamins from fruit and vegetables. All work well as a meal in themselves, but they could also be scaled down and served with snacks or pastries, ideal for picnics or buffets. Many of the salads won't wilt in the way that leafy salads do, so they can be packed in lunch boxes.

## NOTES FOR YOUR STORECUPBOARD
◆

- ◆ Wild rice is an aquatic grass with a wonderful nutty flavour that can be very well appreciated when the rice is cold.
- ◆ Bulgar wheat is a partially processed grain that only needs to be soaked for minutes before it is ready to serve.
- ◆ Tiny Puy lentils are my favourite pulse for salads. They have a delicious flavour and a pretty blue-green colour, and they hold their shape once cooked.
- ◆ Seeds of all varieties make useful and nutritious additions to salads. Keep on hand sunflower, sesame and pumpkin seeds.
- ◆ Silken tofu makes a delicious dairy-free mayonnaise.

## TIPS FOR NO-FUSS SALADS
◆

- ✔ grains and beans soak up more flavour if dressed whilst still warm
- ✔ toasting nuts or seeds for a few minutes in a dry pan or in the oven brings out their flavour
- ✔ if you are planning a buffet, fewer ingredients in each salad means more variety overall
- ✔ ring the changes by preparing the fruit or vegetables differently – grating, cutting in chunks, or shaving fine strips using a mandolin or peeler

# Goat's Cheese and Asparagus Salad with New Potatoes and Salsa Verde

♦ gluten free

♦ sugar free

♦ nut free

♦ not suitable for freezing

350 g/12 oz asparagus
450 g/1 lb small new potatoes
6 tablespoons salsa verde
250 g/8 oz goat's cheese
mixed salad leaves including some fresh basil leaves
1–2 tablespoons freshly shaved Parmesan

### SALSA VERDE
♦

The proportions for this sauce can vary according to taste. As a rough guide, for 150ml (¼ pint) of olive oil, finely chop 50g (2oz) of herbs (basil, oregano, marjoram or parsley) and add to the oil. Then mix in some lemon juice, a crushed or chopped clove of garlic, and season well. For speed, make the sauce in a blender or food processor.

### PARMESAN SHAVINGS
♦

Take these from a piece of Parmesan using a mandolin or a potato peeler.

Although the main ingredients in this salad are cooked, it still has a fresh feel and look. I like to use a soft goat's cheese that has a distinctive tang. Serve this salad with crusty granary or sunflower bread and butter.

♦ Trim the asparagus and steam for 8–10 minutes or until tender. Leave to cool.

♦ Cook the new potatoes in boiling water until tender. Drain and mix with the salsa verde while still warm. Cut the cheese into 8 slices.

♦ Arrange the asparagus, potatoes and cheese on a bed of mixed salad leaves. Garnish with Parmesan shavings.

# Bulgar Wheat Salad with Pine Kernels and Tomato Vinaigrette

Bulgar wheat makes a great salad base, but it does need a powerful dressing to counteract its blandness. A fresh tomato vinaigrette does the trick. This is such an easy salad that I make large quantities for parties. If there is any left over it keeps well until the next day.

◆ Roast the pine kernels in the oven preheated to 200°C/400°F/gas 6 for 2–3 minutes or until just golden brown.

◆ Mix the bulgar wheat and salt in a bowl and pour over the boiling water. Stir in lightly, then leave to soak for about 15 minutes. Most of the water should be absorbed, but if the grain seems a little wet, drain well. Add the spring onions, cucumber, red and yellow peppers and the roasted pine kernels to the soaked wheat and mix well.

◆ For the dressing, pour boiling water over the tomatoes, leave for several minutes and then drain. Peel and chop roughly, removing the seeds. Place the chopped tomatoes in a blender and add all the remaining dressing ingredients except the oil. Process until smooth. Add the oil and process again until the dressing is quite creamy. Season to taste. Toss into the bulgar wheat salad.

♦ sugar free
♦ dairy free
♦ not suitable for freezing

50 g/2 oz pine kernels
150 g/5 oz bulgar wheat (or cracked wheat)
$\frac{1}{4}$ teaspoon salt
150 ml/$\frac{1}{4}$ pint boiling water
3 spring onions, diced
$\frac{1}{2}$ cucumber, diced
1 red pepper, diced
1 yellow pepper, diced

*For the dressing*
250 g/8 oz ripe tomatoes
1 tablespoon balsamic vinegar
4 sun-dried tomatoes (packed in oil), chopped
2 cloves garlic, peeled
1 teaspoon dried thyme
1 teaspoon dried marjoram
2 tablespoons olive oil
salt and pepper

# Wild Rice Salad with Sunflower Seeds, Watercress and Egg

♦ sugar free
♦ not suitable for freezing

150 g/5 oz wild rice
250 g/8 oz carrot, grated
25 g/1 oz sunflower seeds
2 sticks celery, sliced
1 large bunch of watercress
2 eggs, hard boiled and sliced
8-10 tinned artichoke hearts, sliced

*For the dressing*
4 tablespoons sunflower oil
2 tablespoons orange juice
1 tablespoon balsamic vinegar
salt and pepper

Wild rice blends very well with hard-boiled egg and artichoke hearts, making a nutritious salad that is full of colour and flavour as well as interesting textures. Serve with some separate bowls of olives, cherry tomatoes and cubes of feta.

♦ Mix the dressing ingredients together and season to taste. Cook the wild rice in twice its volume of water for 35–40 minutes. Drain if necessary, then pour the dressing over the warm rice. Leave to cool.

♦ Mix in the grated carrot, sunflower seeds and celery. Line a bowl or dish with watercress and pile on the wild rice salad. Top with slices of hard-boiled egg and artichoke hearts.

# Oriental Salad

This is a light salad yet packed with nutrients. The bean sprouts are a particularly good source of vitamins, and the peanuts and omelette strips provide protein.

♦ not suitable for freezing

◆ For the omelette strips, beat the eggs with the soy sauce. Using a little oil, make two or three thin omelettes. Leave to cool, then cut into strips.

◆ Mix the dressing ingredients together.

◆ Roast the peanuts in the oven preheated to 200°C/400°F/gas 6 for 3–4 minutes, then chop coarsely. Set aside.

◆ Blanch the sugar snap peas in boiling water for 1 minute, then drain and cool. Mix with the yellow pepper and bean sprouts. Pour over the dressing and mix well.

◆ Garnish the salad with the omelette strips, coriander and peanuts just before serving.

*Illustrated overleaf*

*For the omelette strips*
4 eggs
½ teaspoon soy sauce
vegetable oil for frying

*For the dressing*
grated zest and juice of 1 lime
½ teaspoon salt
1 teaspoon brown sugar
2 tablespoons sunflower oil

50 g/2 oz peanuts
250 g/8 oz sugar snap peas
1 yellow pepper, sliced
250 g/8 oz mixed bean sprouts
2 tablespoons chopped fresh coriander

BEAN SPROUTS
◆
Mung bean sprouts are the most widely available. They are sweet and tender, but always watch out for ungerminated seeds which can be bullet-hard. Chick pea sprouts have a good crunch, but they should be really fresh or they can be sour. Sweet-tasting alfalfa sprouts, whilst a super source of vitamins, are better as a garnish for salad as they have such a fine texture they can get easily lost when mixed with other ingredients

# Mexican Salad Platter

◆ gluten free

◆ sugar free

◆ nut free

◆ dairy free

◆ not suitable for freezing

250 g/8 oz cauliflower florets
250 g/8 oz green beans, chopped
1 x 400 g/14 oz tin mixed beans,
drained and rinsed
1 red onion, finely sliced
1 crisp lettuce such as iceberg
250 g/8 oz cherry tomatoes

*For the dressing*
50 ml/2 fl oz olive oil
juice of ½ lemon
¼ teaspoon cayenne pepper
1 teaspoon cumin seeds, toasted
1 teaspoon fresh thyme
2 cloves garlic, crushed

Mexican food can be put together very easily, to make tempting and substantial salad meals. You can buy or make marinated olives and guacamole, and serve it all with some tortilla chips and a bowl of soured cream or a mixture of soured cream and plain yoghurt.

◆ Make the dressing by mixing all the ingredients together and season with salt and pepper to taste.

◆ Steam the cauliflower and green beans for about 5 minutes, then mix with the tinned beans. Pour over the dressing, toss and leave to cool.

◆ Before serving, add the sliced onion, torn lettuce leaves and cherry tomatoes and toss again.

# Avocado and Fruit Salad

◆ sugar free

◆ nut free

◆ dairy free

◆ not suitable for freezing

1 red pepper, sliced,
1 large ripe avocado, chopped,
1 large papaya, chopped,
juice of ½ lime
2 tablespoons chopped
fresh coriander

This light fruit and vegetable mix also works well with a Mexican-style salad.

◆ Prepare the pepper. Peel and chop the avocado and pawpaw. Mix with the pepper, then pour over he lime juice and toss in the coriander.

# Puy Lentil Salad

This is a robust salad with great earthy flavours sharpened with garlic, mint and yoghurt. It travels well, so is excellent for picnics. Its lentil base means it is full of protein and vital minerals such as iron. As it is dense in texture, I like to serve it with light salad ingredients such as fresh tomato slices, raw celery and carrot sticks and leaves of Cos lettuce. There are varieties of Puy lentils that cook in under 10 minutes, so keep a check when cooking, because if the lentils are too soft this salad will have no texture.

◆ Rinse the lentils, put in a large pan of water and bring to the boil. Simmer for 20–25 minutes or until just tender. Drain and cool.

◆ Grind the walnuts and garlic in a food processor. Add the vinegar and water and blend again to make a paste. Add the oil. Stir in the yoghurt, spring onions and mint.

◆ Mix the lentils into the dressing. Season to taste. Serve at room temperature.

◆ gluten free
◆ sugar free
◆ not suitable for freezing

250 g/8 oz Puy lentils
75 g/3 oz walnut pieces
1 clove garlic, finely chopped
1 tablespoon white wine vinegar
4 tablespoons water
2 tablespoons olive oil
400 ml/14 fl oz plain Greek
yoghurt or thick set yoghurt
3 spring onions, finely chopped
4 tablespoons finely chopped
fresh mint
salt and pepper

# Roast Sweetcorn and Marinated Tofu Salad

◆ sugar free

◆ dairy free

◆ not suitable for freezing

1 packet regular tofu
4 tablespoons soy sauce
1 x 2.5 cm/1 in piece of root
ginger, finely grated
1 tablespoon sesame oil
250 g/8 oz baby sweetcorn
2 tablespoons sunflower oil
2 tablespoons chopped
fresh rosemary
salt and pepper
16 cherry tomatoes, sliced
4 spring onions, chopped
shredded Chinese leaves

Chunky well-flavoured pieces of tofu contrast well with succulent roast sweetcorn in this robust salad. Serve it as a light lunch with rice cakes or make it into a more substantial meal by adding a rice salad and some bought spring rolls and roasted cashew nuts.

◆ Cut the tofu into bite-sized pieces. Mix the soy sauce and ginger, add the tofu and leave to marinate for at least 2 hours.

◆ Remove the tofu from the marinade and put it on a large baking sheet. Sprinkle with the sesame oil. Bake in the oven preheated to 200°C/400°F/gas 6 for 10–15 minutes. Leave to cool.

◆ Toss the sweetcorn with the sunflower oil and rosemary. Season well. Spread on a baking sheet lined with baking parchment and roast for 12–15 minutes. Leave to cool, then chop each sweetcorn in thirds.

◆ To assemble the salad, mix the tofu and sweetcorn with the cherry tomatoes and spring onions. Line a bowl with shredded Chinese leaves and pile the tofu salad in the middle.

# EXPRESS EATING

MY EVENING ROUTINE HAS CHANGED CONSIDERABLY since having children. My sons are still at the stage of needing tea between 5 and 6 pm, and we aim for a bedtime of around 8. Frequently I come downstairs at 8 pm and think, right, supper, I want it now! I would say that the recipes in this chapter have definitely been inspired by necessity. Whilst many of you reading this may not be recovering from putting children to bed, you may well be dashing in at the end of a hectic day, wanting a tasty and nutritious meal as quickly as possible.

Two of the recipes in this chapter can be prepared, cooked and served in under 15 minutes. The rest, with practice, take less than 15 minutes to prepare. Apart from the potato dish, most of the recipes cook in 15–20 minutes. They don't need much in the way of accompaniments: a steamed vegetable or quick leafy salad will suffice, or, of course, something more elaborate if you wish.

**NOTES FOR YOUR STORECUPBOARD**
◆

◆ As these recipes are mostly made from fresh ingredients, these are what to have in your refrigerator: eggs, goat's cheese, crème fraîche and mozzarella cheese.
◆ A tin of lentils is a great standby.

**TIPS FOR NO-FUSS EXPRESS EATING**
◆

✔ look at the time-saving tips on page 15
✔ many of these dishes can easily be scaled down for one or two
✔ many of the grain dishes on pages 103–112 are quick to prepare and cook, as are the recipes for stir-fry and sauté dishes on pages 75–86

# Mediterranean Fritatta

◆ gluten free

◆ sugar free

◆ nut free

◆ not suitable for freezing

350 g/12 oz potatoes, peeled
3 tablespoons olive oil
1 onion, sliced
2 cloves garlic, crushed
10 sun-dried tomatoes
(packed in oil), sliced
6 tinned artichoke hearts, sliced
1 red pepper, chopped
6 eggs
salt and pepper

In many Mediterranean countries, there is a tradition of making thick, flat vegetable omelettes, known variously as tortilla, kuku or fritatta. These make good, lively coloured supper dishes. Despite the variety of vegetables used, be sure to season the egg mixture well before cooking, as otherwise the result will be disappointingly bland. Serve this with crusty bread and a simple tomato salad or steamed green beans.

◆ Parboil the potatoes for 10 minutes, then drain, cool slightly and cut into thick slices.

◆ Heat the oil in a frying pan and fry the onion and garlic until golden. Add the potato slices and fry until tender. Add the sun-dried tomatoes, artichoke hearts and red pepper and fry for a further 2–3 minutes. Spread out the vegetables in the pan.

◆ Beat the eggs and season well. Increase the heat under the pan to high and pour in the egg mixture. Cook for a minute or two, then reduce the heat and cook for 5–10 minutes or until the frittata is golden brown on the base and set. Serve immediately, cut into wedges.

# Hot Mushrooms with Goat's Cheese

This can be ready on the table in less than 15 minutes. It is a delicious mixture of sauté mushrooms and goat's cheese melted into a rich sauce. Bread and a green salad are good accompaniments, but if you have a little more time, serve with couscous or new potatoes and Italian Tomato Salad with Balsamic Vinegar (page 32).

- ♦ gluten free
- ♦ sugar free
- ♦ nut free
- ♦ not suitable for freezing

25 g/1 oz butter
1 onion, finely chopped
1 clove garlic, crushed
450 g/1 lb mushrooms,
thinly sliced
salt and pepper
175 g/6 oz goat's cheese
3 tablespoons finely chopped
fresh parsley
2 tablespoons chopped fresh basil
3 tablespoons crème fraîche

◆ Melt the butter in a large frying pan, add the onion and garlic and cook gently until soft. Add the mushrooms and season well. Cook over a high heat for about 2 minutes, stirring.

◆ Add the remaining ingredients and stir well to make a sauce. Cook until heated through. Check the seasoning, then serve hot.

# Individual Cheese Popovers

◆ sugar free
◆ nut free
◆ not suitable for freezing

2 eggs
125 g/4 oz plain flour
300 ml/½ pint milk
large pinch of salt
½ teaspoon paprika
75 g/3 oz cheese, grated

*For the sauce*
1 tablespoon sunflower oil
1 shallot, finely chopped
50 g/2 oz green beans
1 red pepper, diced
4 baby sweetcorn, chopped
250 g/8 oz button mushrooms, sliced
2–3 tablespoons crème fraîche
1 tablespoon chopped fresh parsley

These popovers are made from a rich batter similar to that for Yorkshire pudding. Do make sure the oven is hot before you start to bake. There are lots of sauces you could serve with these popovers – mushroom or cheese, for example – but when time is short I like them with this simple vegetable mixture moistened with crème fraîche. For the popovers, use cheddar or any other well-flavoured cheese.

◆ Whisk together the eggs, flour and a little of the milk to make a smooth paste. Then gradually add the remaining milk, whisking all the time to make a smooth batter. Whisk in the salt and paprika. Oil or grease 12 deep muffin or bun tins and heat in the oven preheated to 190°C/375°F/gas 5 for about 5 minutes or until very hot. Remove the tins from the oven and quickly pour in enough batter to fill each tin about half full. Sprinkle on the grated cheese, then cover with the remaining batter. The tins should now be about two-thirds full. Bake for 20 minutes or until well risen and light yet crisp.

◆ Meanwhile, for the sauce, heat the oil in a saucepan and fry the shallot until soft. Add all the remaining vegetables and cook on a high heat, stirring, to draw out the juices from the mushrooms. Turn the heat down and cook until the vegetables are just tender. Mix the crème fraîche with the parsley and stir into the cooked vegetables. Keep warm on a low heat.

◆ When the cheese popovers are cooked, serve immediately with the vegetable sauce.

# Stuffed Tomatoes with Feta and Almonds

Couscous mixed with feta and almonds makes a simple savoury filling for tomatoes. These can be served with a green salad or green vegetable, and also go well with the Potato Wedges Baked with Herbs (page 47).

◆ Roast the almonds in the oven preheated to 200°C/400°F/gas 6 for 4–5 minutes or until golden brown. Shake the pan once or twice during roasting so the almonds brown evenly.

◆ Soak the couscous in the salted boiling water for 5 minutes. Drain if necessary.

◆ Cut a lid from each tomato and scoop out the seeds and central flesh. Mix the couscous with the toasted almonds, crumbled feta, celery, parsley, mint and oil. Season well. Pile the filling into the tomato shells and top with the lids. Bake at 190°C/375°F/gas 5 for 15–20 minutes.

♦ sugar free
♦ not suitable for freezing

50 g/2 oz flaked or chopped
blanched almonds
75 g/3 oz couscous
$\frac{1}{4}$ teaspoon salt
200–250 ml/7–8 fl oz
boiling water
4 large tomatoes
125 g/4 oz feta cheese, crumbled
2 sticks celery, finely diced
2 tablespoons chopped
fresh parsley
2 tablespoons chopped fresh mint
1 tablespoon olive oil
salt and pepper

# Courgette Gratin

♦ gluten free
♦ sugar free
♦ nut free
♦ not suitable for freezing

4 large courgettes, trimmed
1 onion, finely chopped
1 clove garlic, crushed
2 tablespoons olive oil
250 g/8 oz button
mushrooms, sliced
6 sun-dried tomatoes
(packed in oil), chopped
1 red pepper, diced
2 tablespoons tomato purée
vegetable stock or water
1 teaspoon chopped
fresh rosemary
1 teaspoon chopped
fresh oregano
salt and pepper
50 g/2 oz Cheddar cheese, grated

This is an attractive quick supper dish, good to make when courgettes are plentiful and cheap in the summer months. I serve this with couscous for a complete meal.

◆ Make a slit in the courgettes, then microwave on high for 6–8 minutes or until fairly soft. Alternatively, steam them. When cooled, slice in half lengthways and scoop out the central flesh and seeds with a teaspoon. Place the courgette shells in a single layer in a lightly oiled large ovenproof dish.

◆ Whilst the courgettes are cooking, prepare the filling. Cook the onion and garlic gently in the oil until soft but not coloured. Add the mushrooms, sun-dried tomatoes and red pepper and cook until soft. Stir in the tomato purée and 4–5 tablespoons stock or water or enough to make the filling quite moist. Cook for 3–4 minutes. Add the herbs and season well.

◆ Spoon the filling into the courgettes, spreading it all over the surface, and then sprinkle with the grated cheese. Bake in the oven preheated to 190°C/375°F/gas 5 for 20 minutes.

# Roast Vegetables with Tomato Coulis

This simple dish can be made with a variety of vegetables in season. Peppers work well, as do baby artichokes or thick slices of field mushrooms. For a light supper serve the roast vegetables with good rustic bread and a mixed leafy green salad. For a more substantial meal accompany with rice or couscous. Wild Mushroom Soup with Cream and Wine (page 25) would make a good starter.

◆ Season 4 tablespoons of the olive oil, then toss with the vegetables so that the pieces are lightly coated with oil. Spread the aubergine, sweetcorn and courgettes on a large baking sheet, and the tomato halves on a separate baking sheet. Roast in the oven preheated to 200°C/400°F/gas 6 for 20–25 minutes, until soft and well-browned.

◆ Roast the pine kernels for 2–3 minutes or until just beginning to brown. Set aside.

◆ Scrape all the roast tomatoes into a blender and add the remaining olive oil, the garlic and herbs. Blend until smooth. Season to taste.

◆ Arrange the roast aubergine, sweetcorn and courgettes on a platter or individual plates and pour over some of the tomato coulis. Scatter the pine kernels on top. Serve immediately.

*Illustrated overleaf*

◆ gluten  free
◆ sugar free
◆ dairy free
◆ not suitable for freezing

6 tablespoons olive oil
salt and pepper
1 medium aubergine, cubed
175 g/6 oz baby sweetcorn
4 courgettes, sliced
350 g/12 oz plum tomatoes, halved
50 g/2 oz pine kernels
1 clove garlic
1 teaspoon fresh thyme or marjoram

### TOMATO COULIS
◆

This tomato coulis is a very useful quick sauce for pasta as well as steamed green vegetables such as broccoli or fine green beans. If you make it in advance, heat through gently; do not boil or you will lose some of the fresh flavour.

# Lentil Refritos

♦ gluten free
♦ sugar free
♦ nut free
♦ dairy free
♦ not suitable for freezing

4 tablespoons olive oil
1 onion, very finely chopped
2 tomatoes, chopped
1 clove garlic, crushed
1 x 400 g/14 oz tin lentils,
drained
salt

I have to ration myself making this dish as it is so more-ish. The ingredients are very humble, but in combination they cannot be bettered. This makes a good supper dish served with crusty bread and some salads, but I also take it on picnics and include it in buffets. As a plus point (I hope), I must add that these lentils are very popular with children.

♦ Heat 2 tablespoons of the oil and fry the onion until it is quite brown and crisp.

♦ Add the tomatoes and garlic and cook for 3–4 minutes or until the tomatoes begin to soften.

♦ Add the lentils and the remaining oil and heat through. Season well with salt and serve hot or at room temperature.

# Stuffed Field Mushrooms with Mozzarella

Field mushrooms have a succulent yet robust texture and make a very good quick supper dish. This simple stuffing needs the minimum of preparation and a slice of mozzarella provides a finishing touch. Serve with a salad and crusty bread for a complete meal.

◆ sugar free
◆ nut free
◆ not suitable for freezing

◆ Wipe the field mushrooms and remove the stalks. Chop these finely and set aside.

◆ Heat the oil in a frying pan and fry the onion and garlic until soft. Add the chopped mushroom stalks and cook for 2–3 minutes. Put the onion mixture in a food processor and add the remaining ingredients (except the mozzarella). Process until finely chopped. Season to taste.

◆ Pile the filling into the mushrooms and top each with a slice of mozzarella. Place on a baking tray and bake in the oven preheated to 190°C/375°F/gas 5 for 15 minutes. Serve hot.

4 large field or open-cap mushrooms
2 tablespoons olive oil
1 onion, finely chopped
2 cloves garlic, crushed
4 teaspoons chopped sun-dried tomatoes (packed in oil)
125 g/4 oz black olives, pitted
50 g/2 oz breadcrumbs
4 tablespoons chopped fresh parsley
salt and pepper
125 g/4 oz mozzarella

# Potato Gratin Agenaise

- ♦ gluten free
- ♦ sugar free
- ♦ nut free
- ♦ not suitable for freezing

200 ml/7 fl oz crème fraîche
4–6 tablespoons milk
700–900 g/1½–2 lb potatoes,
peeled and thickly sliced
salt and pepper
1 teaspoon chopped fresh thyme
2 tablespoons grated Cheddar
cheese

This dish is very simple but rich and is extremely quick to prepare. True, it takes a bit of time to cook, but this mostly happens unattended. Serve it with a contrasting vegetable or salad, or, for a special occasion, use it as an accompaniment for a pastry dish or casserole.

♦ Mix the crème fraîche with the milk. Lightly oil a shallow ovenproof dish, and put in half the potato slices. Season well and pour over half the crème fraîche mixture. Sprinkle with a little of the thyme. Repeat with the remaining potatoes, crème fraîche and thyme. Season again.

♦ Cover the dish with foil and bake in the oven preheated to 180°C/350°F/gas 4 for 45 minutes. Then remove the foil and sprinkle over the grated cheese. Bake for a further 30 minutes or until the cheese is golden brown and the potatoes are tender. Serve hot.

# COOKER-TOP QUICKIES

THIS CHAPTER CONCENTRATES ON STIR-FRYING and sautéing, two techniques ideal for fuss-free cookery as they are fast, easy and mostly use only one pan. Best of all they are suitable for many combinations of vegetables.

The principle of stir-frying is all in the name – you must stir and fry at the same time so that the food cooks evenly and quickly. A wok is the ideal pan to use as its shape keeps the vegetables in while you toss and stir them, although a deep-sided frying pan could also be used. For ingredients that need a little longer to cook, you can add liquid or a sauce towards the end of cooking to provide a final burst of extra-hot steam.

Stir-fries composed entirely of vegetables can make a nutritious meal if sprinkled with sesame seeds and served with a carbohydrate such as rice (brown basmati is good), or even couscous as long as the stir-fry isn't too dry. For real speed accompany with instant noodles which take only about 3 minutes to cook. Japanese soba noodles are particularly delicious. I also add protein with nuts, particularly cashew nuts and pine kernels, or chunks of tofu and Quorn, marinated to boost the flavour.

Sautés are similar to stir-fries except that they are made in a traditional sauté pan rather than a wok. Usually the ingredients are quickly sautéed in butter or oil to seal in the flavour, then the heat is reduced, liquid is added and the vegetables are left to simmer, to finish the cooking.

## NOTES FOR YOUR STORECUPBOARD
◆

◆ It is useful to have some soy sauce (shoyu or tamari) as well as dry sherry, rice wine (mirin) and sesame oil which makes a great last minute flavouring. Miso, the soya bean paste, is also very useful.
◆ Some instant noodles merely need soaking rather than cooking.
◆ Soba noodles, made from buckwheat, make a tasty change from plain wheat noodles.

## TIPS FOR NO-FUSS STIR-FRIES AND SAUTÉS
◆

✔ when stir-frying, prepare all the vegetables first, cutting them into even pieces so they will cook in roughly the same time
✔ single-handled woks are easier to manage
✔ a sauté pan should have a well-fitting lid, high sides so you can stir the food round without it spilling out, and a heavy base so that the ingredients don't burn

# Stir-fry Mushrooms with Spiced Tofu

♦ sugar free
♦ nut free
♦ dairy free
♦ not suitable for freezing

1 packet regular tofu
1 teaspoon ground cumin
1 teaspoon ground coriander
1 teaspoon turmeric
¼ teaspoon cayenne pepper
3 tablespoons sunflower oil
1 shallot, finely chopped
2 cloves garlic, finely chopped
350 g/12 oz oyster
mushrooms, sliced
350 g/12 oz shiitake
mushrooms, sliced
175 g/6 oz sugar snap peas or
mange touts, cut into thirds
juice of 1 lemon
salt or soy sauce and pepper

This robust stir-fry, with its aromatic flavours, makes a delicious quick supper dish. Serve it with couscous, bulgar wheat or noodles.

♦ Cut the tofu into bite-sized cubes. Mix together the spices and 2 tablespoons of the sunflower oil. Toss in the tofu and leave to marinate for at least 1 hour.

♦ Heat the remaining oil in a wok and quickly stir-fry the tofu, with all the residue of the marinade, until the spices have released their aroma and the tofu is hot. Remove from the wok. Add a little more oil if necessary, then briefly stir-fry the shallot and garlic. Add the mushrooms and peas and stir-fry over a high heat until the mushrooms are well-coloured and soft. Return the tofu to the pan and heat through. Sprinkle with the lemon juice and season, adding a little soy sauce if you wish. Serve immediately.

# Chinese Stir-fry with Omelette and Asparagus

If you prepare the thin omelette strips in advance, the remainder of this stir-fry is very quick. You can use a variety of noodles, but those that only need soaking obviously cut out one more stage of preparation.

◆ sugar free
◆ not suitable for freezing

350 g/12 oz instant noodles
2 tablespoons groundnut or sunflower oil
2 eggs
salt and pepper
1 shallot, finely chopped
2 cloves garlic, finely chopped
1 chilli pepper, de-seeded and chopped
175 g/6 oz baby asparagus, chopped
350 g/12 oz mange touts, sliced diagonally
2 teaspoons sesame oil
1–2 tablespoons soy sauce
2–3 tablespoons vegetable stock or water
snipped fresh chives to garnish

◆ Soak the noodles in boiling water, according to the directions on the packet.

◆ Heat a little of the groundnut oil in a small frying pan. Beat 1 egg and season it, then pour into the frying pan. Cook until the egg sets into a thin omelette. Turn out and leave to cool. Make a second omelette with the other egg. Cut the omelettes into thin strips.

◆ Heat 1 tablespoon groundnut oil in a wok and quickly stir-fry the shallot, garlic and chilli. Add the asparagus and mange touts and stir-fry for 3–4 minutes. Drain the noodles and add to the wok with the sesame oil, soy sauce to taste and stock or water to moisten. Heat through, tossing well to mix, then serve garnished with the omelette strips and snipped chives.

# Stir-fry Vegetables with Soba

◆ sugar free
◆ nut free
◆ dairy free
◆ not suitable for freezing

75 g/3 oz dried shiitake mushrooms
4 tablespoons rice wine or sherry (see box below)
2 tablespoons soy sauce
1–2 teaspoons miso
1 tablespoon sunflower oil
1 shallot, finely chopped
2 large carrots, cut into shavings with a peeler
250 g/8 oz fine green beans
350 g/12 oz soba noodles

**MISO**
◆
Miso comes in a variety of strengths, from the very dark black hatcho miso to milder paler varieties. You can blend miso with water to make instant stocks for sauces and soups, or use it sparingly as a spread on bread.

**RICE WINE**
◆
If you can't get rice wine or mirin, sherry can be substituted but is not as sweet, so you may want to add a pinch of sugar

Soba noodles are lighter and less starchy than wheat noodles. In Japan, the traditional sauce for them is made with fish stock. My recipe uses a mushroom stock with miso, which yields a pleasant salty flavour. It is absolutely delicious.

◆ Soak the mushrooms in lukewarm water to cover for about 10 minutes or until soft. Drain, reserving 250 ml/8 fl oz of the mushroom stock. Slice the mushrooms thinly.

◆ Add the rice wine, soy sauce and miso to the mushroom stock. Set this sauce aside.

◆ Have ready a large pan of boiling water for the noodles.

◆ Heat the oil in a wok and quickly stir-fry the shallot. Add the mushrooms, carrots and beans and stir-fry for 4 minutes. Meanwhile, cook the noodles in the boiling water for 4 minutes. Drain.

◆ Pour the sauce over the vegetables and then toss in the noodles. Serve straightaway.

# Stir-fry Noodles with Sesame and Miso

This dish can be made with fresh thick noodles or dried thin noodles, either soba or udon. It is almost a Japanese equivalent of a sauté as the vegetables are lightly cooked and then finished off by being briefly simmered in the sauce. The end result is moist and full of flavour.

◆ Mix together the ingredients for the sauce and set aside.

◆ Cook the noodles in boiling water for 3–4 minutes, then drain and toss with the sesame oil.

◆ Heat the sunflower oil in a wok and quickly stir-fry the garlic and spring onions. Add the shredded cabbage and stir-fry until just wilted. Turn down the heat. Pour on the sauce, add the noodles and heat through, tossing to mix together. Serve immediately, sprinkled with the sesame seeds.

◆ sugar free
◆ dairy free
◆ not suitable for freezing

350 g/12 oz noodles
1 teaspoon sesame oil
2 teaspoons sunflower oil
2 cloves garlic, finely chopped
8 spring onions, finely chopped
400 g/14 oz spring cabbage or
pak choi, finely shredded
2 tablespoons sesame seeds,
lightly toasted and crushed

*For the sauce*
300 ml/½ pint hot water
2 tablespoons miso
4 tablespoons rice wine or sherry
(see box opposite)
2 tablespoons soy sauce
1–2 teaspoons wasabi paste
1–2 teaspoons hijiki seaweed

**HIJIKI**

Hijiki is a type of seaweed, which is very nutritious. It is sold dried and will keep for months. It only needs to be softened and lightly cooked.

**WASABI**

Wasabi is a type of Japanese horseradish and is very hot and fiery. It is available as a pale green powder or as a paste in tubes.

# Stir-fry Marinated Quorn with Water Chestnuts and Pak Choi

♦ not suitable for freezing

350 g/12 oz Quorn pieces
1 tablespoon sunflower oil
2 spring onions, chopped
300 g/10 oz tinned water
chestnuts, sliced
400 g/14 oz pak choi,
coarsely chopped

*For the marinade*
3 tablespoons dark toasted
sesame oil
3 tablespoons soy sauce
1 tablespoon sunflower oil
1 teaspoon honey
1 teaspoon concentrated
apple juice
juice of ½ lime
6–8 drops of Tabasco sauce
2 spring onions, finely chopped
2 tablespoons chopped
fresh coriander
pepper

This stir-fry has a wonderful mixture of textures and flavours: the Quorn is chewy and quite dry whilst the water chestnuts are crisp and the pak choi soft and moist. Serve this with either rice or noodles.

♦ Prepare the marinade by mixing all the ingredients together. Add the Quorn pieces and leave for 30 minutes to 1 hour. Remove from the marinade with a slotted spoon.

♦ Heat the oil in a wok and stir-fry the Quorn until it is well coloured; remove and set aside. Stir-fry the spring onions briefly, then add the water chestnuts and pak choi. Keep stirring until the pak choi is just becoming soft. Put back the Quorn and heat through. Serve immediately.

# Cashew and Bean Sprout Stir-fry with Three-coloured Vegetables

This is quick, colourful and nutritious as well as lending itself to many variations. I like to include bean sprouts as they are moist and succulent. Other combinations that work well with the cashews are yellow pepper, mange tout and carrot; fine green beans, baby plum tomatoes and mushrooms; asparagus; red pepper and carrot; or sugar snap peas, shiitake mushrooms and baby sweetcorn.

◆ Heat the sunflower oil in a wok and quickly stir-fry the garlic and cashew pieces until golden. Add all the vegetables and continue stir-frying until they are just tender but still crisp.

◆ Mix together the soy sauce, sherry, lemon juice and sesame oil and pour this over the vegetables. Toss the mixture so that it is all well-flavoured, then serve immediately.

◆ sugar free
◆ dairy free
◆ not suitable for freezing

1 tablespoon sunflower oil
1 clove garlic, chopped
125–175 g/4–6 oz cashew nut pieces
350 g/12 oz bean sprouts
1 red pepper, thinly sliced
250 g/8 oz baby sweetcorn, roughly chopped
250 g/8 oz courgettes, cut in sticks
2 tablespoons soy sauce
2 tablespoons dry sherry
juice of ½ lemon
2 teaspoons sesame oil

*Illustrated overleaf (right)*

# Green Bean and Sweetcorn Sauté

♦ gluten free
♦ sugar free
♦ dairy free
♦ not suitable for freezing

50 g/2 oz hazelnuts
2 tablespoons olive oil
2 cloves garlic, sliced
250 g/8 oz green beans,
halved crosswise
250 g/8 oz baby
sweetcorn, halved crosswise
50 ml/2 fl oz vegetable stock
or water
salt and pepper

This is a light colourful dish that works well both as a quick supper or lunch served with rice or noodles. It also makes a good accompaniment to risotto and pastry dishes such as the Spinach and Feta Quiche (page 114) or Spiced Lentil and Almond Filo Pie (page 117).

♦ Roast the hazelnuts in the oven preheated to 190°C/375°F/gas 5 for 5–6 minutes. Leave to cool, then rub off the skins. Chop coarsely.

♦ Heat the oil in a sauté pan and cook the sliced garlic over a low heat until soft. Increase the heat and add the green beans and sweetcorn. Fry for 2–3 minutes, stirring to make sure the vegetables are coated with oil. Pour on the stock or water. Cover the pan, reduce the heat and cook for 5–6 minutes or until the vegetables are just tender.

♦ Toss in the chopped hazelnuts and season well. Serve hot.

*Illustrated on previous pages (left)*

# Ten-Minute Standby Supper

I often make this simple supper. Despite the speed – it can just about be prepared and cooked in 10 minutes, which includes getting the accompanying couscous ready – it is a nutritious meal. This serves 2. For 4 people just double the quantities, but note that it will take just a bit longer to make. You can, of course, vary the combination of vegetables.

◆ Put the couscous into a bowl, add a pinch of salt and cover with the boiling water. Leave to soak whilst preparing the stir-fry.

◆ Heat 1 tablespoon of the oil in a wok and stir-fry the red onion over a high heat. Add the red pepper, courgettes and pine kernels and stir-fry for about 3 minutes. Finally, add the mushrooms and stir-fry until quite soft. Stir in the pesto and season to taste.

◆ Fluff up the couscous with a fork, adding the remaining olive oil. Pile on to plates and top with the stir-fry vegetables.

◆ sugar free
◆ not suitable for freezing

150 g/5 oz couscous
salt and pepper
200 ml/7 fl oz boiling water
3 tablespoons olive oil
1 red onion, chopped
1 red pepper, cut in thin slices
2 courgettes, sliced
75 g/3 oz pine kernels
175 g/6 oz cup
mushrooms, sliced
1–2 teaspoons pesto sauce

### PESTO
◆

Ready-made pesto sauce is widely available, but does vary enormously in terms of flavour. If you have a plentiful supply of basil in the summer, make your own pesto. Grind some pine kernels with basil leaves and garlic, then add a good-quality olive oil. You can then add Parmesan cheese, sun-dried tomatoes or cashew nuts. The final consistency should be thick and fairly smooth. Whether home-made or shop-bought, pesto should be kept in the refrigerator once opened.

# Sauté Florets with Almond Sauce

♦ gluten free
♦ sugar free
♦ dairy free
♦ not suitable for freezing

250 g/8 oz leeks, chopped
250 g/8 oz broccoli florets
250 g/8 oz cauliflower florets
1 tablespoon sunflower oil
50 g/2 oz flaked almonds

*For the sauce*
25 g/1 oz ground almonds
300 ml/1/2 pint vegetable stock
2 tablespoons chopped
fresh parsley
1 teaspoon creamed horseradish
salt and pepper

Although this is not strictly a sauté, I think it fits in well with the theme of this chapter. Nut sauces, particularly ones made from almonds or cashews, are very creamy and rich. They can turn a lightweight vegetable sauté into a nutritious meal that only takes minutes to make. Other vegetable combinations work well here too, such as broccoli and carrot.

♦ First prepare the sauce. Using a blender or food processor, process the ground almonds with the stock, parsley and horseradish. Pour the sauce into a small saucepan and bring to the boil, stirring. Cook for 4–5 minutes or until thickened, then season well.

♦ Prepare all the vegetables, trying to keep them a similar size. Heat the oil in a sauté pan, add all the vegetables and toss over a high heat for 2 minutes. Reduce the heat slightly and add the flaked almonds. Keep stirring the vegetables and cook until just tender. This takes 5–6 minutes.

♦ Pile the vegetables into a warmed dish and top with the almond sauce. Serve immediately.

♦ As an alternative, try this almond sauce with boiled new potatoes for an attractive side dish.

# PASTA

HOW DID WE EVER MANAGE before discovering the wonders of pasta? There was that great British nursery dish, macaroni cheese, but for a long time it didn't seem to occur to anyone to serve macaroni with anything else. Now pasta is available in a vast array of colours, flavours, shapes and sizes, even down to Batman and Robin and Thomas the Tank Engine. It is not just the form of pasta that is so versatile, but the fact that it can combine with a seemingly endless number of sauces – thick, thin, creamy, chunky, they all work well.

Lasagne is the basis of one of the best and most appealing vegetarian dishes, and in this chapter I have included a couple of lasagne recipes. Whilst not a huge hassle to make, they are probably the most time-consuming recipes in this book! However, I think they are worthwhile, being really popular and wholesome. To save effort, several elements can be prepared ahead. A friend of mine always makes two lasagne at a time and freezes one – perhaps a spare lasagne dish should be on everyone's Christmas list.

In addition to lasagne there are recipes for other pasta shapes and some for polenta. At the end of the chapter you'll also find recipes for sauces that go with pasta and polenta.

### NOTES FOR YOUR STORECUPBOARD
◆

- ◆ It almost goes without saying that a wide range of dried pasta shapes is a boon for a busy cook.
- ◆ Keep maize meal in stock to make polenta.
- ◆ A chunk of good Parmesan in the refrigerator is a very useful standby – with a dash of olive oil you have a simple but delicious accompaniment to pasta

### TIPS FOR NO-FUSS PASTA
◆

- ✔ pasta cools down very quickly, so heat the plates and have the sauce ready too
- ✔ a pasta pan with an inner basket is useful for draining pasta quickly
- ✔ chunky sauces work best with pasta shapes such as shells or penne, whilst fine pasta strands need to be coated with a smooth sauce
- ✔ if you have left-over pasta and a sauce, combine the two in an ovenproof dish, cover with grated cheese and bake until hot

# Lasagne with Mushrooms and Quorn

♦ sugar free
♦ nut free
♦ suitable for freezing

150–175 g/5–6 oz sheets of
spinach lasagne
2–3 tablespoons freshly grated
Parmesan

*For the mushroom and Quorn sauce*
2 tablespoons olive oil
1 onion, finely chopped
1 clove garlic, crushed
350 g/12 oz Quorn mince
1 red pepper, finely chopped
2 sticks celery, finely chopped
250 g/8 oz button
mushrooms, sliced
1 x 400 g/14 oz tin
chopped tomatoes
2 teaspoons chopped
fresh marjoram
1 bay leaf
salt and pepper

*For the white sauce*
25 g/1 oz butter or
sunflower margarine
25 g/1 oz wholemeal flour
450 ml/¾ pint milk

Whilst this is a very easy dish to make and assemble, there are two sauces involved so leave yourself enough time or make them ahead. The joy of lasagne is that it really needs no accompaniment other than a simple leaf salad.

◆ To make the mushroom and Quorn sauce, heat the oil in a saucepan and gently cook the onion and garlic for 4–5 minutes. Add the Quorn and cook for 5 minutes, stirring occasionally. Add the red pepper, celery and mushrooms, stir and cook for 5 minutes. Finally, add the tomatoes and herbs. Bring to the boil, then simmer, uncovered, for 30–40 minutes. Season to taste.

◆ To make the white sauce, melt the butter or margarine in a saucepan. Sprinkle over the flour, stir well and cook for 1 minute. Gradually add the milk, stirring constantly. Bring to the boil, then simmer for 3–4 minutes.

◆ If the sheets of lasagne need to be cooked, prepare according to the instructions on the packet. Otherwise, if using no-cook lasagne, either cover the sheets with boiling water and drain, or moisten the sheets with hot water, prior to using.

◆ To assemble, put a little of the mushroom and Quorn sauce on the bottom of an oiled ovenproof dish. Cover with a layer of lasagne, then coat with a little white sauce. Continue making layers, ending with white sauce. Sprinkle the Parmesan over the top. Bake in the oven preheated to 180°C/350°F/gas 4 for 25–30 minutes.

# Lasagne with Roast Vegetables and Ricotta

I love the flavour of roast vegetables in this lasagne, and I find they are quite a hassle-free part of this appetising dish.

◆ Toss the vegetables in seasoned olive oil, then arrange in a single layer on a baking sheet. Roast in the oven preheated to 200°C/400°F/gas 6 for 20–25 minutes or until soft and well-browned. Mix the roast vegetables into the tomato sauce.

◆ To make the white sauce, warm the milk and add the peppercorns, onion, bay leaf and thyme. Leave to infuse off the heat for 15 minutes. Melt the butter in a saucepan, add the flour and stir over a gentle heat for 2 minutes. Strain the milk and add to the roux, stirring. Bring to the boil, stirring constantly, and simmer for 2–3 minutes or until the sauce thickens.

◆ If the sheets of lasagne need to be cooked, prepare according to the instructions on the packet. Otherwise, if using no-cook lasagne, either cover the sheets with boiling water and drain, or moisten the sheets with hot water, prior to using.

◆ To assemble the dish, place a little of the roast vegetable and tomato sauce mixture on the bottom of a large ovenproof dish. Cover with 2–3 sheets of lasagne, spread over half of the remaining vegetable and tomato sauce and dot with half the ricotta. Add a little of the white sauce. Repeat, using up the rest of the ricotta. Finish with sheets of lasagne covered with the remainder of the white sauce. Sprinkle with the grated Parmesan. Bake in the oven preheated to 180 °C/350 °F/gas 4 for 25–30 minutes or until browned on the top.

◆ sugar free
◆ nut free
◆ suitable for freezing

300–450 ml/$\frac{1}{2}$–$\frac{3}{4}$ pint Easy Tomato Sauce (page 98)
6–8 sheets of lasagne
200 g/7 oz ricotta
1–2 tablespoons freshly grated Parmesan

*For the roast vegetables*
1 aubergine, thickly sliced
1 red pepper, sliced
2 courgettes, thickly sliced
1 onion, halved and thickly sliced
olive oil
salt and pepper

*For the white sauce*
450 ml/3/4 pint milk
6 peppercorns
1 onion
1 bay leaf
1 sprig of fresh thyme
40 g/1$\frac{1}{2}$ oz butter
25 g/1 oz plain flour

**RICOTTA**
◆
Ricotta doesn't melt and spread out when heated in the way many cheeses do, so be sure to dot it round evenly, in fairly small lumps.

# Spinach Tagliatelle with Button Mushrooms and Hazelnuts

♦ sugar free

♦ not suitable for freezing

50 g/2 oz hazelnuts
4 tablespoons olive oil
300 g/10 oz button mushrooms, finely sliced
2 cloves garlic, crushed
salt and pepper
300–350 g/10–12 oz spinach tagliatelle
10–25 g/½–1 oz butter
3–4 tablespoons finely chopped fresh parsley
freshly grated Parmesan to serve

A simple sauté of succulent vegetables works very well with pasta and makes a change from lashings of sauce. I serve this with a tomato salad.

♦ Roast the hazelnuts in the oven preheated to 200°C/400°F/gas 6 for 5–6 minutes. Rub off the skins and chop coarsely.

♦ Heat the oil in a frying pan and fry the mushrooms with the garlic on a high heat until well browned. Season well. Add the hazelnuts and fry for a few more minutes.

♦ Cook the pasta in boiling salted water until just tender. Drain and toss with the butter, then add the cooked mushroom mixture and parsley and toss well. Serve immediately with a separate bowl of grated Parmesan.

# Wholemeal Pasta Shells with Summer Vegetables in a Cream Sauce

I think a selection of bright green summer vegetables makes a perfect colour combination with wholemeal pasta. Ring the changes with this recipe by using broccoli or cauliflower florets or broad beans.

◆ sugar free
◆ nut free
◆ not suitable for freezing

300–350 g/10–12 oz wholemeal pasta shells
300 ml/½ pint double cream
1 shallot, finely chopped
125 g/4 oz green beans, sliced
125 g/4 oz shelled fresh peas
125 g/4 oz courgettes, sliced
1–2 tablespoons finely chopped fresh mint
salt and pepper

◆ Cook the pasta in a large pan of boiling salted water for 10 minutes or until just tender.

◆ Meanwhile, heat the cream with the shallot in a large pan. Bring to the boil, then leave to simmer gently while you prepare the vegetables. Steam or microwave the vegetables until just tender. Drain well. Mix the vegetables into the cream sauce.

◆ Drain the pasta and quickly mix into the cream sauce. Add the fresh mint. Season well. Serve immediately.

◆ For a dairy-free version, simply steam the vegetables of your choice, toss the pasta with well-seasoned olive or walnut oil and toss in the vegetables. Top with some toasted nuts.

# Spaghetti with Smoked Cheese

♦ sugar free

♦ nut free

♦ not suitable for freezing

2 eggs
300 ml/½ pint single cream
4 tablespoons finely chopped
fresh parsley
125 g/4 oz smoked cheese,
grated
salt and pepper
300–350 g/10–12 oz spaghetti or
other fine pasta

This is a quick rich sauce with plenty of flavour. Use it to coat a fine pasta such as spaghetti or tagliatelle. As the pasta will already be starting to cool when tossed in the sauce, be sure to have piping hot plates ready for serving. This needs little more than a serving of salad to make a great supper.

♦ Beat the eggs with the cream in a large bowl. Stir in the parsley and grated cheese and season well.

♦ Cook the pasta in a large pan of boiling salted water for 10 minutes or until tender. Drain well, immediately add to the egg and cream mixture and toss to mix. The heat of the pasta should cook the eggs, but, if necessary, return the whole mixture to the pan, set over a gentle heat and toss thoroughly with two forks so that the eggs cook. Serve immediately.

# Pasta with Sauté Spinach and Shallots

Despite this dish having three stages it can be prepared, cooked and on the table in less than 15 minutes. It is important to fry the breadcrumbs until crisp as they then absorb the juices from the spinach and give the dish an interesting texture. I like the colour combination of spinach with wholemeal pasta, but a plain or egg pasta would work as well. This dish really needs nothing with it, although you could serve a tomato salad or some sauté mushrooms if you have time. A bowl of freshly grated Parmesan is also a nice addition.

♦ sugar free
♦ nut free
♦ not suitable for freezing

50 g/2 oz butter
50 g/2 oz breadcrumbs
300–350 g/10–12 oz wholemeal
pasta spirals
2 shallots, finely chopped
1–2 teaspoons Dijon mustard
450 g/1 lb spinach, rinsed
and dried

◆ Melt half of the butter in a frying pan and fry the breadcrumbs until crisp. Set aside.

◆ Cook the pasta in a large pan of boiling salted water until just tender.

◆ Meanwhile, melt the remaining butter in a large saucepan and cook the shallots for 3 minutes or until just soft. Add the mustard and mix in well. Tear or snip the spinach leaves into small pieces and drop them into the pan. Keep the heat high and continue cooking until the spinach is just wilted.

◆ Drain the pasta and toss it with the spinach and shallot mixture, then quickly mix in the breadcrumbs and serve immediately.

*Illustrated overleaf (right)*

# Polenta with Roast Chilli Sauce

♦ gluten free
♦ sugar free
♦ nut free
♦ not suitable for freezing

200 g/7 oz coarse polenta
1.2 litres/2 pints boiling water
1 teaspoon salt
50 g/2 oz margarine or butter
125 g/4 oz mature Cheddar
cheese, grated

*For the sauce*
1 fresh green chilli
2 tablespoons sunflower oil
1 onion, finely chopped
2 cloves garlic, crushed
2 peppers (red or green), diced
1 teaspoon dried oregano
½ teaspoon ground cinnamon
1 x 400 g/14 oz tin chopped
tomatoes
salt and pepper

*Illustrated on previous pages*
*(left)*

Polenta is easy to make and can be prepared well ahead. It works with all sorts of flavours, and its bland nature is ideal for tempering fiery sauces. I serve this with roast vegetables (see recipe on page 89), steamed courgettes or green beans.

◆ To cook the polenta in the conventional way, bring the water and salt to the boil in a large saucepan and slowly pour in the polenta, stirring constantly. Leave the mixture to simmer for 20–30 minutes. To cook the polenta in the microwave, see Deep-fried Polenta, opposite.

◆ Stir in the margarine or butter and pour the mixture into a greased dish. Leave to cool, then cut into small squares.

◆ For the sauce, roast the chilli in the oven preheated to 200°C/400°F/gas 6 for 10 minutes. Leave to cool, then peel and remove the seeds. Chop the flesh finely.

◆ Heat the oil in a saucepan and gently fry the onion and garlic until soft. Add the chilli and diced peppers and cook for 5–10 minutes over a gentle heat. Stir in the oregano, cinnamon and tomatoes. Bring to the boil, then simmer for 20 minutes. Season to taste.

◆ Put the squares of polenta in a shallow ovenproof dish. Spoon over the sauce, then cover with grated cheese. Bake in the oven preheated to 200°C/400°F/gas 6 for 20–25 minutes or until the cheese has melted and browned and the polenta is heated through.

# Deep-fried Polenta

I love the contrasting textures of deep-fried polenta – a crisp outer shell with an almost custard-like middle. Serve this with dips as a filling appetiser for a light meal, or fry in larger pieces, layer in a casserole with Easy Tomato Sauce (page 98) and slices of mozzarella and bake.

- ◆ gluten free
- ◆ sugar free
- ◆ nut free
- ◆ dairy free
- ◆ not suitable for freezing

200 g/7 oz coarse polenta
1.2 litres/2 pints boiling water
1 teaspoon salt
50 g/2 oz margarine or butter
oil for deep frying

◆ To cook the polenta in the microwave, put it in a large bowl, pour over the boiling water, add the salt and stir well. Cook for 8–10 minutes on high heat, stirring several times. To cook the polenta in the conventional way, see Polenta with Roast Chilli Sauce, opposite.

◆ Stir in the margarine or butter and pour into a greased dish. Leave to cool, then cut into small squares.

◆ To fry, heat the oil in a deep pan until very hot. Add a few squares of polenta at a time and fry until golden and crisp. Drain on kitchen paper. Serve hot.

### AN ALTERNATIVE
◆
For an extra crisp finish, dip each square of polenta in beaten egg and then fine cornmeal before deep frying.

# Easy Tomato Sauce

♦ gluten free
♦ nut free
♦ dairy free
♦ suitable for freezing

2 tablespoons olive oil
1 onion, finely chopped
2 x 400 g/14 oz tins chopped tomatoes
1 teaspoon sugar
1 teaspoon salt
1 bay leaf
1–2 cloves garlic (optional)
pepper

There are so many uses for this sauce that I always make it in large quantities. It will keep for at least a week in the refrigerator, or up to six months in the freezer. I use it as a topping for pasta shapes as well as a base for lasagne. It goes well with pastry dishes such as Chestnut Pie with Herbs (page 115) or Stilton and Courgette Strudel (page 116), as well as with barbecue dishes and burgers. Perhaps most important of all, it is very popular with my children.

◆ Heat the oil in a large saucepan and gently fry the onion until translucent. Add the tomatoes, sugar, salt and bay leaf. Bring to the boil, then cover and cook gently for 30 minutes. Discard the bay leaf.

◆ Leave to cool slightly, then whizz, with or without the garlic, in a food processor or blender until very smooth. Check the seasoning.

◆ For a creamy finish, add 1–2 tablespoons olive oil when puréeing the sauce.

◆ Easy Tomato and Mushroom Sauce: After puréeing the sauce, return it to the pan and add 350 g/12 oz thinly sliced mushrooms. Bring to the boil, cover and simmer for 15–20 minutes. Season to taste.

# Zested Lemon Butter with Herbs

If you are really short of time and energy, pasta can be served very plainly, just tossed in olive oil or a flavoured oil such as basil oil. You can also toss it with a little butter and cream to make a richer dish. The third alternative is to toss it in a lemon and herb butter. Make this in advance and store it in the refrigerator where it will keep for up to a week. It will be ample for 350 g/12 oz pasta.

◆ gluten free
◆ sugar free
◆ nut free
◆ suitable for freezing

125 g/4 oz butter, at room temperature
6 tablespoons finely chopped fresh herbs (basil, thyme, marjoram, sorrel or rocket)
grated zest of 1 lemon
1 clove garlic, crushed
pepper

◆ Soften the butter, then add the remaining ingredients and cream again. Chill.

◆ Toss with freshly cooked pasta and serve immediately.

# Melted Dolcelatte Sauce with Shallots

♦ gluten free
♦ sugar free
♦ nut free
♦ not suitable for freezing

25 g/1 oz butter
2 shallots, chopped
200 g/7 oz mascarpone
125 g/4 oz Dolcelatte
1 tablespoon chopped fresh tarragon
salt and pepper

This quick and simple recipe turns pasta into something sumptuous. All you need with it is a green salad and fresh fruit to follow.

♦ Melt the butter in a small saucepan and sauté the shallots for 3–4 minutes or until just softened.

♦ Stir in the mascarpone and Dolcelatte and allow to melt gently. Mix in the tarragon and season well. Serve over freshly cooked pasta.

# Fennel Sauce with Cream and Saffron

Saffron gives this rich sauce a marvellous golden hue. I like to pour it over spinach- or tomato-flavoured pasta. Do chop the fennel finely so that it blends well with the cream mixture and yet still retains some texture. Depending on your choice of pasta, you could serve this with buttered spinach or broccoli or grilled tomatoes and a sauté of sliced field mushrooms and red onion.

- ◆ gluten free
- ◆ sugar free
- ◆ nut free
- ◆ not suitable for freezing

$\frac{1}{2}$ teaspoon saffron strands
25 g/1 oz butter
2 shallots, finely chopped
1 clove garlic, crushed
300 ml/$\frac{1}{2}$ pint double cream
250–300 g/8–10 oz bulb fennel, finely chopped
2 teaspoons lemon juice
salt and pepper

◆ Cover the saffron with 2 tablespoons boiling water and leave to soak to make an infusion. Melt half of the butter in a large saucepan and gently cook the shallots and garlic until soft. Add the cream and the saffron infusion. Bring to the boil, then simmer gently until reduced by about one-quarter.

◆ In a separate pan, melt the remaining butter and gently braise the fennel until quite soft, adding a little water or stock if necessary. Pour the cream sauce over the braised fennel and stir well. Season with the lemon juice, salt and pepper.

◆ Serve with freshly cooked pasta.

# Fresh Plum Tomato and Mushroom Sauce with Wine

- ♦ gluten free
- ♦ sugar free
- ♦ nut free
- ♦ dairy free
- ♦ suitable for freezing

2 tablespoons olive oil
1 onion, chopped
2 cloves garlic, crushed
2 sticks celery, chopped
250–300 g/8–10 oz shiitake
mushrooms, chopped
45 ml/3 tablespoons red wine
450 g/1 lb fresh plum tomatoes,
peeled and chopped
6 sun-dried tomatoes (packed in
oil), chopped
1 teaspoon dried marjoram
1 tablespoon concentrated
apple juice
salt and pepper

**CONCENTRATED APPLE JUICE**

♦

Concentrated apple juice is a useful storecupboard ingredient. Dilute it to drink, but use undiluted to sweeten acidic sauces as well as to add a fruity flavour to vinaigrette dressings.

This is a well-textured sauce that goes with small pasta shells or spirals. It makes a good supper or lunch dish, served by itself or with a little salad and cheese or fruit to follow.

♦ Heat the oil and gently cook the onion and garlic until soft. Add the celery and mushrooms and cook over a high heat until beginning to soften. Add the wine. Bring to the boil, then turn down the heat and cook for 10 minutes.

♦ Add the chopped fresh and sun-dried tomatoes, the marjoram and apple juice and mix well. Cover the pan and leave to simmer gently for 20–25 minutes. Season well and serve hot.

# RICE AND GRAINS

GRAINS IN ONE FORM OR ANOTHER are a staple food throughout the world. They are a valuable part of the diet as they can contain useful amounts of fibre and protein as well as being good sources of iron and Vitamin B. They are cheap, easy to cook and, above all, versatile – they can be partnered with numerous ingredients, sweet or savoury.

If I analyse our evening meals, I find grains crop up in one form or another at least 4 or 5 times a week. I love rice in all its forms, whether as an accompaniment to spicy curry or stir-fry vegetables or, as in the recipes in this chapter, cooked with other ingredients to make a fuss-free main dish. Apart from rice, I also use a lot of couscous and bulgar wheat.

In this chapter you'll find recipes for a pilaff and risotto, including a microwave version of risotto that works very well. There are also some simple ideas for using couscous and bulgar wheat.

### NOTES FOR YOUR STORECUPBOARD
♦

- ♦ It is worth having a range of rice in stock so you can use the most appropriate, e.g special short-grain rice for risotto or fragrant basmati rice for a pilau.
- ♦ Most grains have a very long shelf life.
- ♦ For gluten-free grains, buy millet and buckwheat. Buckwheat has a stronger flavour than rice, but can work well with robust dishes. Millet is good for making risotto as it becomes quite creamy once cooked.
- ♦ Nuts combine well with grains, in both flavour and texture, as well as providing a complementary protein. Have a variety on hand, such as cashew nuts, walnuts, pine kernels and hazelnuts.

### TIPS FOR NO-FUSS RICE AND GRAINS
♦

- ✔ soaking rice will speed up the cooking process
- ✔ a little saffron or turmeric makes all the difference to the look of a plain grain
- ✔ left-over grains reheat well in the microwave
- ✔ don't buy nuts in vast quantities as they can go stale quite quickly

# Cashew and Saffron Pilaff

♦ gluten free
♦ sugar free
♦ dairy free
♦ not suitable for freezing

250 g/8 oz white basmati rice
450 ml/¾ pint water
3 tablespoons sunflower oil
6 cloves
1 stick cinnamon
1 teaspoon ground cardamom
50 g/2 oz cashew nuts, chopped
1 onion, finely chopped
1 teaspoon saffron threads
25 g/1 oz sultanas
125 g/4 oz shelled fresh or
frozen peas
1 teaspoon salt

I make this aromatic pilaff with white basmati rice as it looks so wonderful when the saffron is added, but you can, of course, use brown basmati rice if you prefer (the cooking time will be a little longer). Serve this pilaff with Spiced Cauliflower with Broad Beans (page 148), with Onion Fritters (page 45) or a simple tomato and cucumber salad.

♦ Put the rice in a bowl and cover with the water. Leave to soak for half an hour. Drain, reserving the water.

♦ Pound the saffron strands in a pestle and morter and infuse in 2 tablespoons of boiling water.

♦ Heat the oil in a saucepan, add the cloves, cinnamon and cardamom and cook, stirring, for 1 minute. Add the chopped cashew nuts and cook for 1 minute or until lightly browned. Add the onion and fry very gently until soft but not coloured. Add the drained rice and mix in thoroughly, coating with the oil. Pour over the reserved water and add the saffron infusion, sultanas, peas and salt. Bring to the boil, stirring frequently, then partially cover the pan and simmer for 10 minutes.

♦ Turn the heat down as low as possible and cook for a further 10 minutes or until the rice is tender and the liquid has been absorbed. Leave to rest covered and off the heat for 5 minutes. Fluff up with a fork before serving.

### SAFFRON
♦

Saffron, the red-yellow stamens of the saffron crocus, is the most expensive spice in the world. Although it can be bought in powdered form, you are more likely to get the real thing if you buy strands. One teaspoon of strands is roughly equivilent to just over ¼ teaspoon of ground saffron

# Sweet and Sharp Bulgar Pilaff

Capers and lemon add a sharp contrast to sweet raisins in this simple pilaff. Serve it with plain yoghurt, feta cheese or a tahini dressing (page 38) plus a green or tomato-based salad to make it into a light meal. It is also good served with a vegetable extra such as Ratatouille with Lemon and Yoghurt (page 149) or with a casserole.

♦ sugar free
♦ dairy free
♦ not suitable for freezing

1 tablespoon olive oil
1 onion, very finely chopped
1 teaspoon ground cinnamon
½ teaspoon turmeric
250 g/8 oz bulgar wheat
600 ml/1 pint vegetable stock
or water
50 g/2 oz raisins
2 tablespoons capers
50 g/2 oz pine kernels
grated zest and juice of 1 lemon
salt and pepper

♦ Heat the oil in a saucepan and cook the onion over a very gentle heat for 10 minutes or until it is really soft. Add the spices, stir and cook for 2–3 minutes. Add the bulgar wheat and cook for 1 minute, stirring.

♦ Pour over the stock and add the remaining ingredients. Bring to the boil, then simmer for 10–15 minutes or until the bulgar wheat is soft.

*Illustrated overleaf (with feta cheese)*

# Cajun Quorn and Rice with White Wine

♦ gluten free

♦ sugar free

♦ nut free

♦ not suitable for freezing

2 tablespoons olive oil
1 onion, chopped
1 clove garlic, crushed
1 fresh green chilli, chopped
2 sticks celery, sliced
1 red pepper, chopped
350 g/12 oz Quorn pieces
250 g/8 oz long-grain brown rice
1 tablespoon tomato purée
400 g/14 oz chopped tomatoes
200 ml/7 fl oz dry white wine
300 ml/½ pint vegetable stock
1 teaspoon dried oregano
salt and pepper

This is a great no-nonsense supper dish. It is very easy to prepare, and if you cook and serve it in the same dish you save on washing up, too. It is a highly nutritious recipe. Serve with a plain green vegetable such as steamed green beans or broccoli or, if you have more time, Baby Spinach with Ginger and Garlic (page 145).

♦ Heat the oil in a large frying pan. Add the onions, garlic and chilli and cook gently for 3–4 minutes or until the onion has softened. Add the celery and red pepper and soften for 2–3 minutes. Stir in the Quorn pieces and rice and cook for a further 2–3 minutes, stirring constantly. Add the tomato purée, tomatoes, wine, stock, oregano and seasoning. Bring to the boil, then simmer for 30–35 minutes or until the rice is cooked and the liquid has been absorbed. Check the seasoning and serve hot.

# Wild Mushroom Risotto

Risotto benefits from being made with good home-made stock, not something always on hand. Wild mushrooms solve this problem – the soaking liquid makes a marvellous stock, and the mushrooms themselves can then be added to the risotto for extra texture and flavour. Stirring the rice during cooking produces the classic creamy quality of risotto. Serve with buttered baby spinach and carrots.

♦ gluten free
♦ sugar free
♦ nut free
♦ not suitable for freezing

10 g/½ oz dried mushrooms, such as ceps (porcini) or trompettes des morts
600 ml/1 pint boiling water
2 tablespoons olive oil
1 onion, chopped
1 clove garlic, crushed
40 g/1½ oz butter
250 g/8 oz arborio rice
½ teaspoon dried thyme
salt and pepper
2 tablespoons freshly grated Parmesan

♦ Cover the dried mushrooms with the boiling water and leave to soak for at least 30 minutes. Drain in a fine sieve set in a bowl. Rinse the mushrooms and chop finely. Strain the mushroom stock through a coffee filter to remove any sediment and reserve.

♦ Heat the oil in a saucepan and gently fry the onion and garlic until soft but not coloured. Add 25 g/1 oz of the butter to the pan and, when melted, add the rice, chopped dried mushrooms and thyme. Stir until the rice is well coated with the butter and oil. Add 150 ml/¼ pint of the mushroom stock. Cook, stirring, until the stock has been absorbed, then add another 150 ml/¼ pint of the mushroom stock. Continue cooking, gradually adding the remaining stock as the previous batch is absorbed. The rice should become tender but still firm, surrounded by a thick creamy sauce. It should take 20–25 minutes to cook overall.

♦ Just before serving, season well and add the remaining butter and the grated Parmesan.

# Microwave Risotto with Carrot and Courgette

♦ gluten free

♦ sugar free

♦ nut free

♦ not suitable for freezing

2 tablespoons olive oil
1 onion, finely chopped
250 g/8 oz arborio rice
2 sticks celery, finely diced
1 litre/1¾ pints vegetable stock
2 carrots, peeled and grated
1 courgette, grated
salt and pepper
25–50 g/1–2 oz butter
2 tablespoons freshly grated
Parmesan

I tried shock-horror tactics on an Italian friend when I told her how I found the microwave useful for making risotto. Far from passing out, she saw the value of creating a delicious creamy rice dish without being tied to the stove for well over half an hour. True, the end result does not have quite the authentic texture of a slowly-stirred risotto but it makes a very acceptable substitute. This particular recipe is one that I make frequently for my children. I also make microwave risotto as supper for grownups when I add finely chopped leeks, mushrooms or fennel.

♦ Cook in a covered dish, on high (600W) throughout.

♦ In a large dish suitable for a microwave, mix the oil and onion. Cook for 1 minute. Stir in the rice and celery and cook for 1 more minute. Stir well again, then pour over the vegetable stock. Cook for 5 minutes. Stir well again, then add the grated carrots and courgette. Cook for a further 4 minutes, and check on the liquid content, adding a little more if necessary. Then cook for a further 4 minutes. Stir again and check if the rice is cooked. If not, cook for a further 2 minutes, adding more liquid if necessary.

♦ Season well and add the butter and Parmesan cheese. Serve immediately with extra Parmesan cheese.

MICROWAVE TIPS
♦
Make sure you know the wattage of your microwave. A 'high' setting may vary from 500–750W. For lower wattage, increase the cooking time. For larger or smaller amounts of food, increase or decrease the cooking time respectively. Always check the food after the minimum suggested cooking time.

# Mushroom and Almond Rice with Chilli

The dark colours of this dish look warm and rich, and the roast chilli adds a fiery hint. This is delicious served with grilled courgettes or steamed green beans and a separate bowl of plain yoghurt.

◆ sugar free
◆ dairy free
◆ not suitable for freezing

1–2 large fresh mild green chillies
2 tablespoons olive oil
1 onion, very finely chopped
2 cloves garlic, crushed
125 g/4 oz button mushrooms, finely chopped
125 g/4 oz long-grain brown rice
125 g/4 oz wild rice
50 g/2 oz blanched almonds, toasted and chopped
600 ml/1 pint boiling vegetable stock or water
2–3 tablespoons finely chopped fresh parsley
salt and pepper

◆ Roast the chillies in the oven preheated to 200°C/400°F/gas 6 for 10 minutes. Leave to cool, then remove the skin and seeds and chop the flesh.

◆ Heat the oil in a saucepan and gently fry the onion and garlic until very soft. Add the mushrooms and cook until softened, then add the chopped chilli, the brown and wild rice and the almonds. Stir well so the rice grains are coated with oil and cook for 2 minutes. Pour over the boiling stock or water. Bring to the boil, then simmer for 25–30 minutes or until the rice is cooked and the liquid has been absorbed. Check on the liquid towards the end of cooking and add more if necessary.

◆ Stir in the parsley and seasoning and serve immediately.

**CHILLIES**
◆
◆ Chillies come in a wide variety of strengths, from scorching-hot to quite mild. Usually the smaller and more compact the chilli is, the more powerful is its heat. Larger chillies range from medium hot to mild. Redder chillies tend to be sweeter than green, and the sweetness can counteract their fire.
◆ Always take care when handling chillies – don't touch your eyes, lips or any other sensitive place until you have washed your hands.

# Spicy Chick Peas with Couscous

◆ sugar free
◆ nut free
◆ dairy free
◆suitable for freezing

2 tablespoons olive oil
1 onion, chopped
2 cloves garlic, crushed
1 teaspoon ground coriander
½ teaspoon ground ginger
¼ teaspoon ground cinnamon
1 green pepper, chopped
1 x 400 g/14 oz tin chick peas, drained
300 ml/½ pint passata
salt and pepper

*For the couscous*
300 g/10 oz couscous
400 ml/14 fl oz boiling water
½–1 teaspoon salt
1–2 tablespoons olive oil

Tinned pulses make a good addition to a grain dish as they add protein as well as colour and texture. They are also very quick to heat through.

◆ Heat the oil in a saucepan and fry the onion and garlic until softened. Add the spices and cook for 1–2 minutes, stirring. Add the green pepper and chick peas and cook for 5 minutes, stirring frequently. Pour over the passata. Bring to the boil, then simmer gently for 10 minutes. Season to taste.

◆ While the sauce is simmering, put the couscous in a large bowl, pour over the boiling water and stir in the salt. Leave to soak for 5 minutes. Drain if necessary, then add the olive oil and fluff up the couscous with a fork just before serving, with the sauce.

# PASTRY AND PIZZA

DESPITE WHAT YOU MAY THINK, making pastry and pizza dough is really simple and doesn't take a lot of time. There are some very easy recipes in this chapter to convince you, and all the fillings I've suggested are quick to make.

Traditional rubbed-in pastries, such as shortcrust for classic pies and quiches, are worth having in every cook's repertoire, and are particularly fuss-free if you use a food processor. Another pastry that is easy to make is choux. It is baked in spoonfuls so there is no rolling out. Filo pastry is one to buy rather than make. Once you have used it a couple of times, I'm sure it will find a permanent place in your freezer, as it is extremely versatile.

Whilst I have gone through phases of buying pizza and pizza bases for convenience, I have to say that home-made is always much better, and making the dough with easy blend yeast is very quick. By making your own pizza dough, you can also choose the type that suits you and your family: a robust wholemeal base for a filling meal, mini pizzas which children love, or a rich almost cake-like base for special suppers and parties. I have suggested a couple of basic toppings, including an idea without tomatoes for those who feel they can never get away from them.

NOTES FOR YOUR STORECUPBOARD
♦
- Dried yeast is sold in both tubs and sachets. Having sachets saves you the bother of measuring out.
- For pastry, you need plain white or wholemeal flour; pizza dough uses strong bread flour, either unbleached white or wholemeal.
- Tins or jars of olives and capers make quick toppings.
- Have filo pastry on hand in the freezer, wrapped in convenient portions

TIPS FOR FUSS-FREE PASTRY AND PIZZA
♦
- pastry can be made in advance and stored in the refrigerator or freezer. Make sure it is properly wrapped so that it won't dry out
- buy filo pastry fresh if possible, then store frozen in smaller, convenient-sized portions
- left-over vegetable mixtures make good fillings for individual filo pies, which are useful for packed lunches
- easy blend dried yeast doesn't have to be dissolved in liquid, but can be added directly to the flour

# Spinach and Feta Quiche

The robust flavours of spinach and feta complement a wholemeal pastry base. I prefer quiche such as this served warm, but cold it could be part of a picnic spread. Serve this with colourful contrasting salads such as tomato or pepper and new potato. For more of a 'snacky' meal, cut the quiche into little wedges and serve with some of the tapas ideas on pages 47–49.

◆ sugar free
◆ suitable for freezing

*For the pastry*
125 g/4 oz wholemeal flour
pinch of salt
2 tablespoons sesame seeds
50 g/2 oz solid vegetable fat
and/or butter, well chilled
1 tablespoon sunflower oil
2–3 tablespoons cold water

*For the filling*
2 tablespoons sunflower oil
1 onion, chopped
350 g/12 oz spinach, rinsed
4 eggs
150 ml/¼ pint single cream
150 ml/¼ pint milk
salt and pepper
150 g/5 oz feta cheese, crumbled
2 tablespoons sesame seeds

◆ Make the pastry by mixing the flour, salt and sesame seeds. Rub in the fat, then add the oil and enough water to bind to a dough. Wrap in cling film and chill for 30 minutes.

◆ Roll out the dough and use to line a 20 cm/8 in flan ring or tin. Bake in the oven preheated to 200°C/400°F/gas 6 for 5 minutes.

◆ For the filling, heat the oil in a large pan and gently fry the onion until soft. Add the spinach and stir-fry over a high heat until wilted and the juices have boiled away. Leave to cool.

◆ Whisk the eggs with the cream and milk and season well. Spread the spinach mixture in the pastry case. Sprinkle over the crumbled feta, then pour on the egg mixture. Scatter the sesame seeds over the top. Return to the oven and bake for 25 minutes. Serve warm.

# Chestnut Pie with Herbs

This is a tasty pie, ideal for special occasions and festive meals. With 'envelope-style' pastry dishes such as this, I prefer to make the pastry with white flour as it is inevitably lighter. If you prefer wholemeal you may need extra water and longer to chill. Both the filling and pastry can be prepared ahead of time. Serve this with Easy Tomato Sauce (page 98) plus Shredded Leeks with Wine and Crème Fraîche (page 145) or Potato Gratin Agenaise (page 74), a steamed green vegetable, and a glazed or roast root vegetable.

◆ For the pastry, mix the flour with the salt in a large bowl. Grate in the fat. Add the lemon juice and just enough water to make a dough. Wrap in greaseproof paper and chill for 30 minutes.

◆ Roll out dough to a long oblong, roughly 36 x 30 cm (14 x 12 ins). Fold up the bottom third, then fold down the top third. Seal the edges and make a quarter turn. Repeat the rolling and folding and then chill again.

◆ For the filling, heat the oil in a frying pan and gently cook the onion, leeks and garlic until very soft. In a large bowl, mix together the chestnuts, walnuts, herbs, and soy sauce and lemon juice to taste. Add the cooked cooled onion and leek mixture and season well.

◆ To assemble, roll out the dough into a large rectangle. Place the filling in the centre. Make diagonal cuts in the dough, about 2.5 cm/ 1 in apart, on either side of the filling. Fold the cut strips over the filling to create an interwoven effect. Tuck in bottom ends. Brush well with 1 egg yolk beaten with a pinch of salt. Bake in the oven preheated to 200°C/400°F/gas 6 for 25–30 minutes. Serve hot.

◆ sugar free
◆ suitable for freezing

*For the pastry*
250 g/8 oz plain flour
½ teaspoon salt
150 g/5 oz solid vegetable fat
and/or butter, frozen for 30
minutes prior to using
1 tablespoon lemon juice
8–9 tablespoons ice cold water

*For the filling*
2 tablespoons sunflower oil
1 onion, finely chopped
2 leeks, finely chopped
2 cloves garlic, crushed
400 g/14 oz cooked dried
chestnuts (see below), chopped
125 g/4 oz walnut pieces,
chopped
6 tablespoons chopped
fresh parsley
4 tablespoons finely chopped
fresh coriander
2–3 tablespoons soy sauce
2–3 tablespoons lemon juice
salt and pepper

**TO PREPARE DRIED CHESTNUTS**
◆
Soak in plenty of water for about 30 minutes, then cook in the same water for 30–40 minutes until soft. To get 400 g/14 oz cooked weight, start with 200 g/7 oz.

# Stilton and Courgette Strudel

♦ sugar free
♦ not suitable for freezing

3–4 tablespoons olive oil
2 medium-sized leeks,
finely chopped
2 cloves garlic, crushed
350 g/12 oz courgettes
4 tablespoons white wine
175 g/6 oz Stilton, crumbled
2 eggs, beaten
2 tablespoons chopped
fresh parsley
salt and pepper
50 g/2 oz melted butter
12 sheets of filo pastry

This is a lovely main dish for a party. Serve it with Potato Wedges Baked with Herbs (page 45), and a salad or a green vegetable.

♦ Heat 1 tablespoon of the oil in a frying pan and gently fry the leeks and garlic for 4–5 minutes. Add the courgettes and continue cooking for 2–3 minutes. Add the wine and cook until most of the liquid has evaporated. Leave to cool.

♦ Crumble the Stilton into a bowl and add the beaten eggs and parsley. Mix in the cooled leek and courgette mixture. Season well.

♦ To prepare the strudel, mix the butter with the remaining olive oil. Brush one sheet of filo with the butter mixture and use to line the bottom and sides of a square ovenproof dish, 20 x 20 cm (8 x 8 ins). Place a second sheet of buttered filo on top. Continue layering the filo until you have a base of 6 sheets. Trim around the top of the dish. Put the vegetable mixture in the dish and level off. Cover with the remaining filo, buttering and layering the sheets as before. Tuck the pastry in around the edges of the dish. Slice through the pastry with a sharp knife to mark into portions.

♦ Bake in the oven preheated to 200°C/400°F/gas 6 for 35–40 minutes or until the pastry is crisp and golden. Turn the oven down a little for the last 10 minutes if the pastry is becoming too brown. Serve hot.

♦ If you add three eggs, this mixture can be used to fill a 20 cm (8 in) pastry case.

### FILO PASTRY
♦

When using frozen filo pastry, be sure that it is completely thawed or it will be very brittle. While working, keep the sheets you are not using covered with a damp tea towel or cloth – filo dries out very quickly and will then be difficult to handle.

# Spiced Lentil and Almond Filo Pie

Feather-light filo pastry is a good foil for earthy lentils, giving you a substantial but not too weighty dish. This make a great cold weather supper served with Easy Tomato Sauce (page 98) or Quick Red Cabbage with Apple (page 150), sauté potatoes and a green vegetable. You can also make minute triangles of filo stuffed with this mixture, which work well for lunch boxes, snacks or children's teas.

♦ sugar free
♦ dairy free
♦ suitable for freezing

2 tablespoons sunflower oil
2 onions, chopped
1 teaspoon ground coriander
1 teaspoon ground turmeric
1 teaspoon ground ginger
125 g/4 oz red lentils
250 ml/8 fl oz boiling water
50 g/2 oz almonds, chopped
juice of ½ lemon
salt and pepper
12 sheets of filo pastry
3–4 tablespoons olive oil

♦ Heat the sunflower oil in a saucepan and gently fry the onions with the spices until very soft. This will take about 10 minutes. Add the lentils and boiling water and stir. Bring to the boil, then cover and simmer on a low heat for 15–20 minutes or until the lentils are soft and the mixture falls to a purée. If it is still a little wet, cook uncovered for a few minutes. Leave to cool, then mix in the chopped almonds, lemon juice and seasoning.

♦ To prepare the strudel, brush one sheet of filo with olive oil and use it to line the base and sides of a square, 20 x 20 cm (8 x 8 in) ovenproof dish. Place another sheet of oiled filo on top. Continue layering the filo until you have a base of 6 sheets. Trim around the top of the dish. Put the lentil mixture in the dish and level off. Cover with the remaining filo, brushing with oil and layering as before. Tuck the pastry in around the edges of the dish. Slice through the pastry with a sharp knife to mark into portions.

♦ Bake in the oven preheated to 200°C/400°F/gas 6 for 35–40 minutes or until the pastry is crisp and golden. Turn the oven down a little for the last 10 minutes if the pastry is becoming too brown. Serve hot or warm.

# Gougère with Leeks and White Wine

♦ sugar free
♦ not suitable for freezing

*For the pastry*
150 ml/¼ pint water
50 g/2 oz butter
50 g/2 oz plain flour, sifted
2 eggs
50 g/2 oz Cheddar cheese, grated
¼ teaspoon prepared mustard

*For the filling*
2 tablespoons olive oil
1 onion, chopped
450 g/1 lb leeks, chopped
4 tablespoons white wine
4 teaspoons pesto sauce
salt and pepper
shavings of Parmesan

Here spoonfuls of choux pastry are arranged in a ring for baking, making a gougère. Be sure to bake the gougère thoroughly, because if not crisp it may sink when removed from the oven. This dish works well with new potatoes and glazed carrots.

♦ For the pastry, put the water and butter in a saucepan and bring to the boil. When boiling and the butter has melted, remove the pan from the heat and shoot in all the flour. Beat until the mixture is very glossy. Beat in the eggs one at a time. Then add the grated cheese and mustard and beat again.

♦ Put the pastry in spoonfuls around the side of a lightly greased 23 cm (9 in) flan dish to form a ring. Bake in the oven preheated to 200°C/400°F/gas 6 for 20 minutes, then reduce the heat to 190°C/375°F/gas 5 and bake for a further 5–10 minutes.

♦ Meanwhile, make the filling. Heat the oil in a frying pan and gently cook the onion until soft but not coloured. Add the leeks and cook for 3–4 minutes, then add the white wine and braise the leeks until just soft. Stir in the pesto and season to taste.

♦ Pile the filling into the centre of the choux pastry ring, garnish with Parmesan shavings and serve immediately.

# Crisp Wholemeal Pizza with Herbs

The first pizza I ever ate in Italy was a metre long and was served cut in squares. I think this is the best way to serve wholemeal pizza, rather than making individual rounds. The base can be rolled very thinly so there is room for plenty of topping. Choose a topping from the recipes on page 121, or make up your own.

◆ sugar free
◆ nut free
◆ dairy free
◆ suitable for freezing

350 g/12 oz strong wholemeal bread flour
1 teaspoon salt
1 packet easy blend dried yeast
1 teaspoon dried thyme
200 ml/7 fl oz warm water
2 tablespoons olive oil

◆ Mix the flour, salt, yeast and thyme in a large bowl. Add the warm water and olive oil and work the mixture into a dough. Knead well until firm and elastic. Return the dough to a clean bowl and cover with cling film or a damp cloth. Leave in a warm place until well risen. Knead again.

◆ Brush a tray measuring about 36 x 30 cm/14 x 12 in with olive oil. Roll or press out the pizza dough to fill the tin. Leave in a warm place for 10 minutes.

◆ Add the topping (see page 121) and bake in the oven preheated to 210°C/425°F/gas 7 for 15 minutes. Reduce the heat to 190°C/375°F/gas 5 and bake for a further 10–15 minutes.

*Illustrated on pages 122–123 (right)*

# Luxury Deep Pan Pizza

♦ sugar free
♦ nut free
♦ suitable for freezing

250 g/8 oz strong white
bread flour
1 teaspoon salt
1 packet easy blend dried yeast
4 tablespoons milk
2 medium eggs, beaten
2 tablespoons olive oil

For a deep pan pizza, you really need an extra special dough, otherwise the pizza will just seem bottom heavy! Luckily a rich dough is just as easy to make, though it works better with a white flour. Serve the pizza on its own or with a selection of salads.

♦ Mix the flour, salt and yeast together in a large bowl. Warm the milk slightly, then add it to the bowl with the beaten eggs and olive oil. Work into a dough and knead well, until firm and elastic. The dough should have a soft, slack consistency; if it is too sticky, just knead in a little more flour. Put the dough in a clean bowl and cover with cling film or a damp cloth. Leave in a warm place until well risen. This can take an hour.

♦ Knead the dough again. Lightly brush a 23 cm/9 in tin or deep flan dish with oil. Put the dough in the tin and press it out to line evenly. Leave to rise for about 10 minutes.

♦ Spread over your choice of topping (see page 121). Bake the pizza in the oven preheated to 210°C/425°F/gas 7 for 15 minutes, then reduce the heat to 190°C/375°F/gas 5 and bake for a further 10 minutes. Serve hot, cut into wedges.

*Illustrated overleaf (left)*

# Rough Tomato Sauce

There are numerous ready-made sauces that certainly take a lot of the effort out of pizza-making, but I still prefer making my own. This tomato sauce is very quick to prepare. It can be left plain, or topped with olives, peppers, pine kernels, cheese or whatever.

♦ sugar free
♦ nut free
♦ dairy free
♦ suitable for freezing

♦ Heat the oil and gently fry the onion and garlic until soft. Add the chopped tomatoes and oregano and stir well. Bring to the boil, then simmer over a moderate heat, stirring frequently, until some of the liquid has evaporated and you are left with a rich pulp. Season to taste.

1–2 tablespoons olive oil
1 onion, finely chopped
1 clove garlic, crushed
1 x 400 g/14 oz tin chopped tomatoes
1 teaspoon dried oregano
salt and pepper

# Onion and Caper Topping

This onion topping is moist and flavoursome, and really works best on its own, without a tomato base.

♦ sugar free
♦ nut free
♦ dairy free
♦ not suitable for freezing

♦ Heat 2 tablespoons of the oil in a frying pan and gently cook the onions for about 10 minutes or until very soft and translucent. Season to taste.

♦ Brush the pizza base with a little of the remaining oil. Spread the onion mixture over the base and then scatter on the capers. Drizzle the rest of the oil on top.

2–3 tablespoons olive oil
2–3 medium onions, cut into thin rings
salt and pepper
2 tablespoons capers

*Both toppings illustrated overleaf*

# Wholemeal Mini Pizzas

◆ sugar free
◆ nut free
◆ bases suitable for freezing

350 g/12 oz half strong
wholemeal and half strong white
bread flour
1 teaspoon salt
1 packet easy blend dried yeast
1 tablespoon olive oil
200 ml/7 fl oz warm water

*For the topping*
chopped tomatoes or Rough
Tomato Sauce for Pizza
(page 121)
grated cheese
selection of vegetables (sliced
button mushrooms, olives, baby
sweetcorn rounds, sliced
peppers) (optional)

These make good snacks or, if you make them one-bite-size, great pre-dinner appetisers. I find a mixed wholemeal and white dough works very well: I have suggested half and half, but you can vary the proportions according to taste.

◆ Mix together the flours, salt and yeast in a large bowl. Add the olive oil and warm water and mix to a dough. Knead well until firm and elastic. Put into a clean bowl, cover with cling film and leave to rise in a warm place.

◆ Knead the dough again, then divide into pieces weighing about 20 g/¾ oz. Roll out each into a disc approximately 7.5 cm (3 ins) diameter. Alternatively, roll out all the dough and cut out discs with a large round cutter. Place the pizza bases on an oiled baking sheet. Spoon a little chopped tomato or tomato sauce on each base and spread out evenly, then top with grated cheese and vegetables, if using. Leave to rise for 10–15 minutes.

◆ Bake in the oven preheated to 210°C/425°F/gas 7 for 12–15 minutes. Eat hot or at room temperature.

# ONE-POT WONDERS

THE TITLE OF THIS CHAPTER REALLY SAYS IT ALL. The recipes here are all different combinations of vegetables, herbs and other flavourings simmered slowly in liquid. The end results, for very little trouble, are tasty, heart-warming meals which can easily do for suppers or be made into something more substantial or even more elegant for entertaining. No wonder most of the world's cuisines feature a stew or casserole, a ragout or tagine.

Whilst the cooking of a one-pot dish may be lengthy, the preparation generally is not. Once the casserole is in the oven it needs very little attention. These sorts of dishes are also simple to present as they do not need an elaborate range of accompaniments. All the recipes in this chapter can be served just with bread, although you might want to add other accompaniments. There are some ideas in the next chapter to make your one-pot wonder even more wonderful.

NOTES FOR YOUR STORECUPBOARD
♦

♦ Try to have in stock a range of beans, peas or lentils to ring the changes. Tinned pulses do not need any preparation, whereas those that have been dried need soaking for a few hours and then cooking until tender in fresh water.
♦ Keep a good selection of spices, stock cubes or powder

TIPS FOR NO-FUSS ONE-POT WONDERS
♦

✔ a handful of bulgar wheat added towards the end of cooking will thicken a thin texture
✔ a handful of chopped fresh parsley or coriander helps bring out the colours of the vegetables if they have become very muted during the long cooking
✔ most casseroles reheat well and are suitable for freezing. Invest in a pan that will allow you to make a large amount at one go, then simply double or treble recipe quantities
✔ a reheated casserole will have a softer texture. Add a cornbread topping or layer of savoury crumble as a contrast
✔ when reheating, keep a check on the liquid content so it doesn't dry out

# Pumpkin Gumbo

♦ gluten free

♦ sugar free

♦ nut free

♦ dairy free

♦ suitable for freezing

2 tablespoons sunflower oil
1 teaspoon cumin seeds
1 onion, chopped
1 clove garlic, crushed
125 g/4 oz okra, halved
175 g/6 oz baby sweetcorn,
chopped
250 g/8 oz green beans,
cut in thirds
450 g/1 lb pumpkin or butternut
squash flesh, diced
1 tablespoon chopped sun-dried
tomatoes (packed in oil)
1 x 400 g/14 oz tin chopped
tomatoes
1 teaspoon dried oregano
1 teaspoon dried thyme
½ teaspoon ground allspice
salt and pepper

Gumbo is a traditional stew from the American south. It usually contains okra, which has a glutinous quality that helps thicken the cooking liquid. I serve this with Corn Bread (page 137), a mixture of brown rice and wild rice or with couscous.

◆ Heat the oil in a large pan and toast the cumin seeds lightly. Add the onion and garlic and cook until soft. Add the okra, sweetcorn, beans and pumpkin and stir well. Cook for 5–7 minutes or until just beginning to soften.

◆ Add the sun-dried tomatoes, tinned tomatoes, oregano, thyme and allspice. If necessary, add a little liquid (the stew should not be too sloppy). Bring to the boil, then cover and simmer for 50–60 minutes or until all the ingredients are very soft. Season to taste.

# Winter Vegetable Hotpot with Herbs

This simple casserole makes a good warming supper dish in the autumn and winter months. I like to cut the vegetables in quite large chunks so that they keep their character once cooked. Serve this with baked potatoes or mashed potatoes. If you add dumplings (see page 141) half way through cooking you can turn the casserole into a more substantial meal.

◆ Heat the oil in a large pan and gently fry the onion until it is soft but not coloured. Add the leeks, celery, carrots, parsnips and swede. Sweat the vegetables for 10 minutes, stirring occasionally.

◆ Add the lentils, herbs and stock and stir to mix. Bring to the boil, cover and simmer for 45–50 minutes or until all the vegetables are tender. Season to taste and serve hot.

◆ gluten free
◆ sugar free
◆ nut free
◆ dairy free
◆ suitable for freezing

2 tablespoons sunflower oil
1 onion, finely chopped
2 leeks, chopped
4 sticks celery, diced
4 medium-sized carrots,
peeled and chopped
2 medium-sized parsnips,
peeled and chopped
250 g/8 oz swede, peeled
and chopped
25 g/1 oz red lentils or
yellow split peas
1 teaspoon chopped
fresh rosemary
1 tablespoon finely chopped
fresh thyme
3 tablespoons finely chopped
fresh parsley
1 bay leaf
300 ml/½ pint vegetable stock
500 ml/16 fl oz passata
salt and pepper

# Three-bean Chilli

♦ gluten free
♦ sugar free
♦ nut free
♦ dairy free
♦ suitable for freezing

3 tablespoons olive oil
2 onions, roughly chopped
2 cloves garlic, crushed
1–2 fresh green chillies,
de-seeded and chopped
1 teaspoon cumin seeds
1 stick cinnamon
2 sticks celery, sliced
3 medium carrots, chopped
1 red pepper, chopped
1x 400 g/14 oz tin red kidney
beans, drained and rinsed
1x 400 g/14 oz tin black eye or
pinto beans, drained and rinsed
50 g/2 oz green lentils,
500 ml/16 fl oz passata
300 ml/½ pint vegetable stock
salt and pepper

Of all the vegetarian casseroles, chilli is one of the most popular. The most successful chillis have plenty of colour and a range of textures, which is easily achieved by using different types of beans and a handful of lentils. Serve with baked potatoes, rice or Corn Bread (page 137), plus a green vegetable or simple salad if you like.

♦ Heat the oil in a large pan and gently fry the onions and garlic until soft but not coloured. Add the chillies, cumin seeds and cinnamon stick and fry for 2 minutes, stirring. Add the celery, carrots and red pepper and cook for 10 minutes, stirring occasionally.

♦ Add the beans and lentils and mix in well. Pour on the passata and stock. Bring to the boil, then cover and simmer for 50–60 minutes. Remove the cinnamon stick, season well and serve hot.

# Puy Lentils and Mushrooms with Red Wine and Shoyu

This is a richly coloured casserole with distinctive, complex flavours, even though the cooking time is so short. Serve with baked potatoes and glazed shallots, steamed carrots or a green vegetable such as broccoli.

♦ sugar free
♦ nut free
♦ dairy free
♦ suitable for freezing

◆ Heat the oil in a large pan and fry the onion and garlic until soft. Add the mushrooms and cook for 10 minutes or until quite soft. Add the lentils and carrots with the wine, soy sauce (shoyu), water and passata. Stir in the herbs. Bring to the boil, then cover and cook for 40–45 minutes or until the lentils are just tender. Add more liquid if necessary. Remove the bay leaf, and season to taste. Serve hot.

2 tablespoons olive oil
1 onion, chopped
2 cloves garlic, crushed
250 g/8 oz chestnut mushrooms, quartered
175 g/6 oz Puy lentils
8 oz carrots, diced
125 ml/4 fl oz red wine
2 teaspoons soy sauce (shoyu)
300 ml/1/2 pint water
4 tablespoons passata
1 bay leaf
1 teaspoon dried thyme
2 tablespoons finely chopped fresh parsley
salt and pepper

*Illustrated overleaf (right)*

# Spiced Tofu and Vegetable Tagine

◆ gluten free

◆ sugar free

◆ nut free

◆ dairy free

◆suitable for freezing

1 tablespoon sunflower oil

1 onion, finely chopped

3 cloves garlic, crushed

1 x 2.5 cm/1 in piece of root ginger, peeled and grated

2 bay leaves

1 teaspoon ground cumin

1 teaspoon ground coriander

½ teaspoon ground cinnamon

2 red peppers, diced

350 g/12 oz green beans, sliced

1 packet regular tofu, cut into bite-sized pieces

1 x 400 g/14 oz tin chopped tomatoes

300 ml/½ pint vegetable stock

2 tablespoons tomato purée

salt and pepper

2–3 tablespoons chopped fresh coriander to garnish

Casseroles such as this North African tagine work really well with an ingredient such as tofu, which can be bland unless cooked with a multitude of spices. In this dish the spices are aromatic rather than hot, and colour comes from the green beans and red pepper. If possible, cook this dish a day ahead so the flavours have time to develop. Serve with couscous, bulgar wheat or rice.

◆ Heat the oil in a large pan and fry the onion, garlic and ginger until softened. Stir in the spices and fry for a few minutes.

◆ Add the red peppers and green beans and cook very gently until just beginning to soften. Add the tofu to the vegetables, then add the tomatoes, vegetable stock and tomato purée and stir well. Bring to the boil. Simmer gently for 50–60 minutes. Season well. Sprinkle with the chopped coriander and serve hot.

*Illustrated on previous pages (left)*

# Quorn Casserole

Quorn, colourful vegetables and herbs make a rich well-flavoured stew, ideal for autumn evenings. It is worth making an extra quantity of this casserole as it can be kept in the fridge for 3–4 days or in the freezer for 1–2 months. Mashed potatoes are a favourite accompaniment, but it also works well with baked potatoes or rice.

◆ Heat the oil in a large pan and gently fry the onion and garlic for 5 minutes. Add the vegetables and Quorn and stir in well. Cook for 10 minutes.

◆ Add the remaining ingredients, except the soured cream, and bring to the boil, stirring frequently. Cover and cook for 45–60 minutes, stirring occasionally. If necessary, add a little more stock. Season to taste. Serve hot, with the soured cream in a separate bowl.

◆ sugar free
◆ nut free
◆ suitable for freezing

2 tablespoons olive oil
1 onion, finely chopped
1 clove garlic, crushed
2 leeks, chopped
1 red pepper, diced
1 x 200 g/7 oz tin sweetcorn
kernels, drained
1 medium aubergine, diced
250 g/8 oz Quorn pieces
1 teaspoon dried oregano
1 teaspoon dried thyme
1 bay leaf
2 teaspoons paprika
1–2 tablespoons tomato purée
1 tablespoon soy sauce
600 ml/1 pint vegetable stock
salt and pepper
150 ml/¼ pint soured cream
(optional)

# Walnut and Olive Pistou

♦ dairy free
♦ suitable for freezing

2 tablespoons sunflower oil
1 onion, chopped
2 cloves garlic, crushed
1/2 teaspoon cumin seeds
½ teaspoon ground cinnamon
2 sticks celery, chopped
2 medium-sized courgettes, sliced
250 g/8 oz green beans,
halved crosswise
25 g/1 oz walnut pieces
2 tablespoons sherry
1 x 400 g/14 oz tin chopped
tomatoes
75 g/3 oz pitted black olives
1 teaspoon dried oregano
1 x 25 g/1 oz slice of bread
salt and pepper

This casserole is easily assembled and quickly cooked. It is ideal for those cool summer evenings when you want a hot meal but nothing too heavy. You could simply serve this with an interesting bread, new potatoes or rice, or, for a richer meal, with Potato Gratin Agenaise (page 74) and a side salad of mixed peppers, roasted or raw.

♦ Heat the oil in a large pan and gently cook the onion with one of the garlic cloves until soft. Add the cumin seeds and cinnamon and cook for 2 minutes. Add the celery, courgettes, green beans and walnuts and cook for 5 minutes. Then add the sherry and bring to the boil. Add the tinned tomatoes, olives and oregano and stir well. Bring back to the boil, then cover and simmer for 40–45 minutes or until all the ingredients are tender.

♦ Meanwhile, spread the second crushed garlic clove over the bread. Bake in the oven preheated to 200°C/400°F/gas 6 for about 10 minutes or until dry, then grind into crumbs. Add to the casserole and cook for a further 5 minutes or so. Season to taste and serve hot.

# ACCOMPANIMENTS

THE SIDE DISHES HERE HAVE BEEN DEVISED to accompany the casseroles and stews in the previous chapter. To make your choice of accompaniment, be guided by the look of your meal and how much time you have: baked potatoes are best not rushed, whereas couscous takes only about 5 minutes.

These accompaniments can be used in other ways, too. For example, a large baked potato can be the basis for a meal served with several of the vegetable extras in the next chapter. Corn bread is delicious with soups as well as salads, whilst rice and couscous also go well with stir-fry dishes.

NOTES FOR YOUR STORECUPBOARD
♦

♦ Keep in stock a range of grains. It is useful to have a choice of rice, couscous or bulgar wheat.

# Crumble Topping

♦ sugar free

♦ dairy free

♦ suitable for freezing

50 g/2 oz wholemeal flour
50 g/2 oz rolled oats
25 g/1 oz sunflower seeds
25 g/1 oz sesame seeds
1 teaspoon chopped fresh thyme
75 g/3 oz sunflower margarine
salt and pepper

A savoury crumble topping is a very easy way to add texture and substance to a stew. The plainest mixture can be made from oats and flour bound together with a little oil, which saves the messy job of rubbing in. That sort of crumble topping is quite crisp and dry, so should be used with a stew that has plenty of spare liquid. The simple crumble topping here can easily be varied by adding chopped blanched almonds or walnuts, chopped fresh parsley or paprika. Grated cheese will ensure that the mixture browns to an appetising golden colour.

♦ Combine the flour, oats, sunflower seeds, sesame seeds and thyme in a large bowl. Rub in the margarine and season well. Sprinkle the crumble mixture over a prepared casserole. Bake in the oven preheated to 190°C/375°F/gas 5 for 30 minutes. Serve hot.

# Corn Bread

Made from golden maize flour, this bread is very easy, just a quick mixing of wet and dry ingredients before baking. This version is made with milk and eggs which gives it a rich, slightly cake-like finish. It goes well with most casseroles but especially those made with warming spices or sweet-flavoured vegetables. Best made and eaten on the same day.

◆ nut free
◆ not suitable for freezing

125 g/4 oz wholemeal flour
125 g/4 oz maize flour
(corn meal)
1 tablespoon caster sugar
2 teaspoons baking powder
½ teaspoon salt
1 teaspoon toasted cumin seeds
2 eggs
250 ml/8 fl oz milk
2 tablespoons sunflower oil

◆ Combine the wholemeal flour, maize meal, sugar, baking powder, salt and toasted cumin seeds in a large bowl.

◆ In a jug, beat the eggs with the milk, then add the oil. Add this liquid to the dry ingredients and mix quickly.

◆ Pour the mixture into a greased tin measuring 20 x 20 cm/8 x 8 ins. Bake in the oven preheated to 200°C/400°F/gas 6 for 20 minutes. Serve cut in squares, either hot or warm.

*Illustrated overleaf, with Red Pepper, Tomato and Tofu Soup (page 24)*

# Simple Spiced Rice

◆ sugar free
◆ dairy free
◆ not suitable for freezing

1 tablespoon sunflower oil
1 small onion, finely chopped
¼ teaspoon chilli powder
½ teaspoon ground coriander
½ teaspoon ground ginger
250 g/8 oz brown basmati rice
600 ml/1 pint boiling vegetable stock or water
1 tablespoon tomato purée
3–4 tablespoons chopped fresh coriander leaves
salt and pepper
wedges of lemon or lime to serve

This dish makes a good accompaniment to casseroles and stir-fries.

◆ Heat the oil in a saucepan and gently fry the onion until soft. Add the spices, mix well and cook for 2 minutes. Add the rice, stir in and cook for 1 minute. Pour over the stock or water. Mix in the tomato purée. Bring to the boil, stirring once or twice. Turn the heat down to a simmer and cover with a well-fitting lid. Cook for 20–25 minutes or until the rice is tender. Check on the liquid near the end of cooking and add a little more if necessary.

◆ Gently stir in the coriander leaves and season to taste. Serve immediately, or leave to cool before eating. Garnish with wedges of lime or lemon.

# Couscous with Pesto

◆ sugar free
◆ dairy free
◆ not suitable for freezing

300 g/10 oz couscous
½–1 teaspoon salt
400 ml/14 fl oz boiling water
1–2 tablespoons olive oil
2–3 teaspoons pesto (optional)

Couscous works particularly well with moist dishes such as stews and casseroles, and is a good choice if you are reheating something quickly and need an instant accompaniment. If you serve it with a drier dish, such as a plain stir-fry, it is worth quickly flavouring the couscous to make it more moist, hence the option of pesto here.

◆ Put the couscous and salt in a large bowl and pour over the boiling water. Leave to soak for 5 minutes. Add the olive oil (and pesto, if using). Fluff up the couscous with a fork before serving.

# Cheese Dumplings with Herbs

These dumplings are not only delicious, but turn any casserole into a nutritious hearty meal. They are virtually a weekly staple in our house when winter arrives. You can vary the herbs and the type of cheese used to complement the casserole. I also like ringing the changes by adding a good pinch of cayenne pepper.

♦ sugar free
♦ nut free
♦ not suitable for freezing

25 g/1 oz soft vegetable margarine
125 g/4 oz wholemeal self-raising flour
50 g/2 oz mature Cheddar cheese, grated
3 tablespoons finely chopped mixed fresh herbs (parsley, rosemary, thyme, sage)
4 tablespoons milk

◆ Rub the soft margarine into the flour, then mix in the grated cheese and herbs. Add the milk and quickly bring the ingredients together into a dough.

◆ Divide the dough into walnut-sized lumps and put into a bubbling casserole or stew. Cover and cook for 20 minutes, occasionally basting with the juices of the stew.

# Baked Potatoes

♦ sugar free
♦ nut free
♦ dairy free
♦ not suitable for freezing

Baked potatoes can be an accompaniment or the basis for a snack or light supper. Cheese, fromage frais or crème fraîche are easy toppings, as is Tahini Dressing (page 38). I also serve them with Roast Vegetables with Tomato Coulis (page 69), or Sauté Mushrooms with Sherry Vinegar (page 49).

♦ For the slow-bake method: Scrub the potatoes, brush lightly with oil and pierce the skin several times. Wrap in foil and bake in the oven preheated to 200°C/400°F/gas 6 for 1½ –2½ hours, depending on the size of the potatoes.

♦ For the quick-bake method: Scrub several large potatoes and chop each in half or thirds. Bake in the oven preheated to 200°C/400°F/gas 6 for 50–60 minutes.

♦ For the microwave method: Scrub the potatoes and pierce the skin. Wrap in kitchen towel. Cook on high (600W) allowing 4–5 minutes per potato. Leave to stand for 5 minutes before serving. Times should be doubled or trebled according to how many potatoes you are cooking (i.e. 8 minutes for 2 potatoes). Cooking times will also depend on the wattage of your microwave. With a larger quantity check towards the end of the cooking time to be sure the potatoes are done, and also rearrange them once or twice during cooking to ensure they cook evenly. If you have time, you can do the initial cooking in the microwave and then finish in the oven. Slightly undercook the potato in the microwave, then remove the kitchen towel and brush with oil. Bake in the oven preheated to 200°C/400°F/gas 6 for 10 minutes to crisp the skin.

# VEGETABLE EXTRAS

WHILST PLAIN STEAMED OR SAUTÉ VEGETABLES are always excellent accompaniments, it is sometimes worth making slightly more elaborate vegetable side dishes if time permits. These can make any meal more special. Or they can be served in their own right with a grain or potato accompaniment as a light meal.

I hope the recipes in this chapter will encourage you to look at familiar vegetables in a new way. Spinach, for example, is often used as part of a dish, such as in a filo pie or a lasagne, but it often isn't at its best if it is watery and plainly served. Quickly cooked with strong flavourings it is quite different. Butternut squash is a great vegetable, but it, too, can be dull if merely boiled. However, when puréed with a little crème fraîche or mascarpone it suddenly comes into its own.

There are recipes here for roasting vegetables, which can work so well with roots as well as the more succulent summer varieties. I've also included an easy pulse recipe, which is handy if you haven't got much in the way of fresh ingredients on hand.

NOTES FOR BUYING VEGETABLES
◆
- ♦ Buy vegetables as fresh as possible, to get the most nutritional value. If you have to buy several days' supply at once, keep them in the fridge. Root vegetables can also be kept in a cool, dark, dry place.
- ♦ Avoid yellowed or wilted greens and bendy carrots.

TIPS FOR NO-FUSS VEGETABLES
◆
- ✔ plain vegetables are best steamed or microwaved to retain the maximum nutritional content. Alternatively, stir-fry or sauté
- ✔ to microwave, cut the vegetables into even-sized pieces, put in a dish and add 2–3 tablespoons water. Cover the dish and cook on high. 250 g/8 oz root or green vegetables take 3–5 minutes depending on the wattage of your oven
- ✔ to steam, make sure the water in the pan is boiling fast before putting in the vegetables on the steamer rack or collapsible trivet
- ✔ to sauté and glaze, melt a little butter or butter and oil in a pan and quickly fry the vegetable pieces. Add sugar if glazing and then water, stock or wine and cook until the vegetables are tender and the liquid virtually boiled away

# Spiced Shallots

♦ gluten free
♦ nut free
♦ dairy free
♦ not suitable for freezing

3–4 tablespoons olive oil
salt and pepper
2 teaspoons coriander seeds,
crushed
700 g / 1½ lb shallots
1 tablespoon red wine vinegar
½ teaspoon Dijon mustard

Shallots, and indeed onions, are wonderful vegetables in their own right, but seem to have been relegated to the job of background flavouring. I like shallots as a side vegetable. Here they are roasted, which keeps them moist and succulent. A little red wine vinegar added at the end prevents them from being too sweet. These make a good accompaniment to pastry dishes or fried ones such as the Cheese and Herb Savouries (page 44).

♦ Pour the olive oil into a bowl, season well with salt and pepper and add the crushed coriander seeds. Toss in the shallots to coat well with the spiced oil. Place the shallots on a shallow baking tray in a single layer and bake in the oven preheated to 200°C/ 400°F/gas 6 for 15–20 minutes or until browned and tender.

♦ Return the shallots to the bowl, add the red wine vinegar and mustard and toss well. Check the seasoning. Serve hot or at room temperature.

# Baby Spinach with Ginger and Garlic

This is a delicious, moist side dish. Serve it hot with couscous or Cashew and Saffron Pilaff (page 104). Cold it is great with a roast aubergine salad (page 28), or Olive and Pepper Strudels (page 41).

◆ Heat the olive oil in a large pan and gently fry the onion and garlic for 3–4 minutes or until just soft. Add the ginger and turmeric and cook, stirring, for 2–3 minutes.

◆ Pat the spinach dry, add to the pan and cook until the leaves have wilted. Mix in the chopped tomatoes and tomato purée and heat through. Season to taste and serve immediately.

*Illustrated overleaf (left)*

◆ gluten free
◆ sugar free
◆ nut free
◆ dairy free
◆ not suitable for freezing

2 tablespoons olive oil
1 onion, finely chopped
1 clove garlic, crushed
1 teaspoon freshly grated
root ginger
½ teaspoon turmeric
250 g/8 oz baby spinach, rinsed
4 tomatoes, peeled and chopped
1 tablespoon tomato purée
salt and pepper

# Shredded Leeks with Wine and Crème Fraîche

Buttery leeks are good with pastry dishes such as Stilton and Courgette Strudel (page 116) or Chestnut Pie with Herbs (page 115).

◆ Melt the butter in a frying pan and gently sauté the leeks until soft. Pour on the wine and cook until the liquid has almost all evaporated. Remove the pan from the heat and quickly stir in the crème fraîche and mustard. Season to taste. Serve immediately.

*Illustrated overleaf (right)*

◆ gluten free
◆ sugar free
◆ nut free
◆ not suitable for freezing

50 g/2 oz butter
350 g/12 oz leeks, shredded
lengthways
6 tablespoons white wine
4–6 tablespoons crème fraîche
1 teaspoon whole grain mustard
salt and pepper

# Spiced Cauliflower with Broad Beans

- ♦ gluten free
- ♦ sugar free
- ♦ nut free
- ♦ not suitable for freezing

350 g/12 oz very small
cauliflower florets
175 g/6 oz frozen broad beans
3 tablespoons sunflower oil
1 onion, chopped
2 cloves garlic, crushed
2 teaspoons cumin seeds, toasted
300 ml/½ pint plain yoghurt
2 tablespoons lemon juice

Cumin, broad beans and cauliflower make a great combination. Here the vegetables are lightly steamed and then quickly mixed with yoghurt to make an instant sauce.

♦ Steam or microwave the cauliflower and broad beans until tender.

♦ Heat the oil in a wide pan and fry the onion and garlic until soft. Add the cooked broad beans and cauliflower florets and the toasted cumin seeds. Mix in and cook for 2–3 minutes. Stir in the yoghurt, 1 tablespoon at a time. Add the lemon juice and season with salt and pepper to taste, then serve immediately.

# Red Beans with Celery

- ♦ gluten free
- ♦ nut free
- ♦ dairy free (optional)
- ♦ not suitable for freezing

2 tablespoons olive oil
1 onion, chopped
2 sticks celery, sliced
1 teaspoon paprika
1 teaspoon ground cumin
1 x 400 g/14 oz tin red kidney
beans, drained
juice of 1 orange
2 tablespoons chopped parsley

There is no reason why pulses cannot be served as an accompanying vegetable. They look colourful and certainly boost the nutritional value of any light meal.

♦ Heat the oil in a saucepan and fry the onion and celery for 5 minutes or until just beginning to soften. Stir in the paprika and cumin and cook for 1 minute. Add the red kidney beans, orange juice and parsley and cook gently for 5–7 minutes or until the beans have heated through. Season well with salt and pepper. Serve hot, with a generous quantity of soured cream if desired.

# Ratatouille with Lemon and Yoghurt

This is a lovely way to make a bit more of a simple vegetable mixture. It works well with the classic ingredients for ratatouille as well as other vegetables, such as red onion, celery or green beans. Serve this with a light grain dish such as a pilaff or a baked potato or as an accompaniment to a filo pie.

◆ Heat 2 tablespoons of the olive oil in a large pan and quickly fry the cubes of aubergine; remove from the pan. Heat the remaining oil in the pan and cook the onion and garlic for 3–4 minutes or until just starting to soften. Add the pepper, courgettes and mushrooms and cook gently for about 10 minutes. Return the cooked aubergine cubes to the pan and stir in the herbs and passata. Season well. Cook for 3–4 minutes, then spoon the mixture into a shallow ovenproof dish.

◆ Mix together the eggs, yoghurt and lemon juice and pour evenly over the vegetables. Bake in the oven preheated to 180°C/350°F/gas 4 for 20 minutes. Serve hot.

◆ gluten free
◆ nut free
◆ dairy free
◆ not suitable for freezing

3–4 tablespoons olive oil
1 aubergine, cubed
1 onion, finely chopped
1 clove garlic, crushed
1 red or green pepper, chopped
4 courgettes, chopped
250 g/8 oz mushrooms, halved or quartered
1 teaspoon dried thyme or marjoram
150 ml/¼ pint passata
salt and pepper
2 eggs, beaten
300 ml/½ plain yoghurt
1–2 tablespoons lemon juice

# Butternut Squash Purée

- ◆ gluten free
- ◆ sugar free
- ◆ nut free
- ◆ not suitable for freezing

1 medium-sized butternut squash (roughly 575g/1¼ lb), peeled
25 g/1 oz butter
1 teaspoon caraway seeds
½ teaspoon dried thyme
salt and pepper
4 tablespoons mascarpone cheese

Butternut squash produces a delicious purée with a marvellous colour, here enriched with creamy Italian cheese. For an extra special purée, use white wine not water.

◆ Split the squash in half and remove the seeds and fibres. Chop into small pieces. Melt the butter in a large saucepan, add the chopped squash and cook gently for about 5 minutes. Pour on a little water and add the caraway seeds, thyme and seasoning. Cook gently for a further 8–10 minutes (in a covered pan), or until the squash is soft., then mash with the mascarpone cheese until smooth. Serve hot.

# Quick Red Cabbage

- ◆ nut free
- ◆ sugar free
- ◆ suitable for freezing

1 tablespoon sunflower oil
1 onion, finely chopped
1 clove garlic, crushed
450 g/1 lb red cabbage
350 g/12 oz cooking apple, peeled, cored and grated
½ tablespoon cornflour
3 tablespoons water
1 teaspoon ground cinnamon
2 tablespoons cider vinegar
1 tablespoon soy sauce
1 tablespoon honey
6 tablespoons passata
4 tablespoons orange juice
salt and pepper

This is a delicious way to prepare red cabbage. It works very well with Spiced Lentil and Almond Filo Pie (page 117) or Potato Gratin Agenaise (page 74), and Cheese and Herb Savouries (page 44).

◆ Heat the oil in a saucepan and quickly fry the onion and garlic. Add the cabbage and fry for 3–4 minutes or until it just begins to soften. Add the apple and fry for 2 minutes, stirring.

◆ Mix the cornflour with the water, then add to the pan with all the remaining ingredients. Stir well. Lower the heat and cook for a few minutes until the sauce thickens and clears. Season to taste and serve hot or cold.

# BARBECUE

WHILST THE BARBECUE IS STILL SOMETIMES SEEN as the preserve of the meat eater, I think everyone finds the taste and colour of barbecued vegetables very appealing. Peppers and onions work particularly well, but many other vegetables are worth a try.

A barbecue is good fun and a lovely way to enjoy food, but it needs to be planned so that it is a leisurely affair for you and your guests. Unless you have an enormous cooking area, the food will have to be cooked in batches, especially vegetables which take up a fair amount of space, so it is important to have several items of non-barbecue food ready – nibbles and snacks to keep your guests or family happy whilst the food is being cooked. The tapas ideas on pages 47–49 work well, as do the light salads and starters on pages 27–38.

In this chapter, I've given recipes for three very different dips which will go well with most barbecued vegetables. They make an impressive trio if served together. You'll also find recipes for a vegetarian kebab using tofu, a substantial baguette with barbecued cheese and a burger recipe. Supplement the barbecue with interesting breads, salads and a variety of cheeses.

### TIPS FOR NO-FUSS BARBECUES
◆

✔ remember that you will need to cook several batches, so have plenty of fuel
✔ prior to barbecuing, toss vegetables in well-seasoned oil or a flavoured one such as walnut oil or chilli oil
✔ cook a contrasting mixture of vegetables each time so that there is a choice whilst waiting for the next batch
✔ there are some very useful gadgets on the market which make cooking and turning vegetables much easier. Look out for hand held grills for flat pieces as well as rectangular wire containers that can hold all those odd shaped pieces

# Wine and Lemon Marinade for Barbecued Vegetables

- ♦ gluten free
- ♦ sugar free
- ♦ nut free
- ♦ dairy free
- ♦ not suitable for freezing

150 ml/¼ pint olive oil
75 ml/3 fl oz white wine
juice of ½ lemon
1 teaspoon grated lemon zest
1 tablespoon chopped
fresh rosemary
1 tablespoon chopped
fresh oregano
4 cloves garlic, thinly sliced
salt and pepper

I think a marinade works particularly well for the more absorbent vegetables such as aubergines and mushrooms as well as for the less succulent such as fennel or squash. This marinade is enough for about 1 kg/ 2 lb of vegetables.

♦ Mix together all the ingredients in a bowl. Stir in the chosen vegetable pieces, cover and leave to marinate for 1–2 hours.

HERE'S HOW TO PREPARE VEGETABLES MOST SUITABLE FOR A BARBECUE:
♦

- ♦ Baby sweetcorn: trim and leave whole if cooking for a platter with dips; cut in half across for threading on to skewers
- ♦ Celery: split sticks lengthways or cut diagonally into pieces. Celery can be dry, so it's a good idea to marinate it prior to cooking
- ♦ Corn on the cob: like potatoes, this can be roasted very successfully in the coals. It takes about 20 minutes and tastes great, even the burnt bits.
- ♦ Courgettes: choose small baby ones that you can simply trim and leave whole, turning whilst cooking. Larger courgettes can be sliced in ovals or chunky sticks, but don't cut them too fine or they will shrivel to nothing
- ♦ Fennel: trim off the feathery tops and quarter or slice thinly lengthways. If possible, marinate before cooking
- ♦ Mushrooms (button and open cup): wipe and leave whole or thickly slice
- ♦ Onions: very sweet varieties of white onion are delicious when barbecued, as is the mild red onion. Trim away the root, leaving enough so that the layers of the onion do not fall apart, then cut in eighths
- ♦ Peppers: red, yellow and orange peppers are deliciously sweet once the juices semi-caramelise, but the green variety can be bitter. Remove the seeds, then cut in half or quarters. For kebabs it is best to cut chunks or slices
- ♦ Potatoes: if you have a decent supply of charcoal you can wrap potatoes in foil and bake amongst the coals. It's a good idea to cook one extra as inevitably one seems to get lost in the fire

# Red Hot Dip

As the recipe title suggests, this is a colourful fiery dip for barbecued vegetables or bread. Instead of using the oven you can roast the ingredients over the charcoal fire, which gives them quite a different flavour.

◆ gluten free
◆ sugar free
◆ nut free
◆ dairy free
◆ not suitable for freezing

◆ Roast the peppers whole in the oven preheated to 200°C/400°F/gas 6 for 30 minutes or until the skins are charred all over. Leave to cool, then peel and remove the seeds.

◆ Roast the garlic cloves for 10 minutes, then peel.

◆ Roast the chilli for about 10 minutes, then put in a plastic bag for 30 minutes to sweat. This will help loosen the skin. Peel the chilli and remove the seeds.

◆ Combine the peppers, garlic, chilli and the remaining ingredients in a blender or food processor and process until smooth. Season to taste.

2 red peppers
6–8 cloves garlic
1 small fresh red chilli
1 teaspoon dried thyme
1 teaspoon white wine vinegar
3 tablespoons olive oil
salt and pepper

# Crème Fraîche and Herb Dip

- ◆ gluten free
- ◆ sugar free
- ◆ nut free
- ◆ not suitable for freezing

200 ml/7 fl oz crème fraîche
5 tablespoons chopped fresh
dill weed
1 spring onion, diced
1 clove garlic, peeled
1 teaspoon cider vinegar
salt and pepper

This simple dip has a marvellous colour and fresh flavour. It makes a cooling contrast to some of the hot combinations I've suggested.

◆ Combine all the ingredients in a small blender or food processor and process until you have a very smooth consistency. Season to taste. Serve at room temperature.

# Toasted Walnut and Olive Dip

- ◆ gluten free
- ◆ sugar free
- ◆ dairy free
- ◆ not suitable for freezing

50 g/2 oz walnut pieces
50 g/2 oz pitted black olives
1 tablespoon tahini or
sesame spread
2 tablespoons walnut oil
1 tablespoon lemon juice
2 cloves garlic, peeled
2–3 tablespoons water
salt and pepper

With its dark woody colour and strong flavour, this dip is delicious with plain barbecued vegetables, and it can also be spread on bread. Use it as well as or instead of the Haloumi cheese when making the baguettes on page 157 – especially useful if you want a dairy-free idea.

◆ Toast the walnuts in the oven preheated to 200°C/400°F/gas 6 for 5–6 minutes or until lightly browned. Leave to cool.

◆Put all the ingredients including the toasted walnuts in a food processor or blender and blend until smooth. Season to taste. If necessary add a little more water to make a dipping consistency.

# Sunflower and Almond Burgers

These burgers are lighter and more colourful than the traditional nut burger. When first made they are quite sticky, so I find it easiest to freeze them and then to cook from frozen. In a frying pan they are quite easy to manage, but barbecuing, you need a wire holder to make turning over easier. Serve these burgers with tomato ketchup or chutney, Spiced Shallots (page 144), barbecued vegetables and a green vegetable or salad. This will make 12 small burgers.

♦ sugar free
♦ suitable for freezing

50 g/2 oz long-grain brown rice
125 g/4 oz ground almonds
50 g/2 oz sunflower seeds
2 tablespoons sunflower oil
1 small onion, finely chopped
2 medium carrots, grated
1 medium egg, beaten
1 tablespoon soy sauce
salt and pepper

◆ Cook the rice in boiling water for 30–35 minutes or until soft. Drain if necessary and leave to cool. Mix the cooled rice with the almonds and sunflower seeds. Add the oil and work it through the mixture with your fingers. Add the chopped onion and carrots and mix well. Add the egg, soy sauce and seasoning and mix until the mixture starts to hold together.

◆ Divide the mixture into 12 portions and shape each into a small burger. Freeze. (If you don't have a freezer, chill them until firm.)

◆ Place the burgers, still frozen, in a wire holder. Barbecue over the charcoal fire for 4–5 minutes on each side. Serve hot.

**Two alternatives**
◆ To fry, heat enough sunflower oil for shallow frying and fry the burgers for 3–4 minutes on each side.

◆ To bake, place the burgers on an oiled baking sheet and bake in the oven preheated to 190°C/375°F/gas 5 for 12 minutes, turning them over half way through.

TIP
◆
If the mixture is too sticky, add a little flour when shaping the burgers

# Marinated Tofu and Vegetable Kebabs

♦ sugar free

♦ nut free

♦ dairy free

♦ not suitable for freezing

1 packet regular tofu, cut into
bite-sized pieces
125 g/4 oz button mushrooms
125 g/4 oz baby sweetcorn,
cut in half across
175 g/6 oz baby plum tomatoes
or cherry tomatoes
1–2 courgettes, thickly sliced

*For the marinade*
juice of 2 limes
2 tablespoons dry sherry
2 tablespoons soy sauce
2 tablespoons concentrated
apple juice
1 tablespoon sesame oil
2 cloves garlic, crushed
1 x 2.5 cm/1 in piece of root
ginger, peeled and grated

Tofu works brilliantly for kebabs. It provides a colour and texture contrast to the vegetables, it provides protein, and it doesn't fall to pieces on the skewer so is easy to handle. The only caveat is that tofu is virtually tasteless so it is vital to marinate it well prior to cooking.

♦ Mix together the ingredients for the marinade in a large bowl. Add the tofu and vegetables and turn carefully in the marinade. Leave for at least 2 hours, longer if possible.

♦ Thread the pieces on to skewers, alternating the tofu with the vegetables. Barbecue over a charcoal fire for 6–8 minutes or until the vegetables are tender and lightly charred and the tofu is heated right through. Baste with the marinade whilst the kebabs are cooking.

**An alternative**
♦ When the weather is not suitable for barbecues, you can cook the kebabs under the grill, or in the oven for 10–12 minutes on 200° C/400° F/ gas 6.

# Barbecued Haloumi Cheese Baguette

Haloumi is a semi-hard Cypriot cheese made from ewe's milk. It is excellent for cooking over a barbecue as it develops in flavour when cooked but doesn't melt away to nothing.

- ♦ sugar free
- ♦ nut free
- ♦ not suitable for freezing

450 g/1 lb Haloumi cheese, sliced
selection of vegetables (mixed coloured peppers, aubergine, field mushrooms, tinned artichoke hearts)
olive oil
4 baguettes, split open
1–2 tablespoons chopped fresh mint

♦ Prepare the vegetables: quarter the peppers, thickly slice the aubergine and field mushrooms and cut the artichoke hearts in half. Brush the vegetables with olive oil and barbecue over a charcoal fire until tender and lightly charred all over, turning regularly during the cooking. Set aside, then barbecue the cheese slices until just heated through. The cheese slices can be put directly on the grill over the coals for about 30 seconds, but the cheese will drip as it melts. I prefer to put the slices on foil, then on the grill. They take longer to heat, but it is less messy.

♦ Lightly toast the cut sides of the baguettes on the barbecue. Top with a mixture of vegetables and slices of cheese. Add a little chopped mint before handing round.

*Illustrated overleaf*

# Rachel's Barbecue Bread

♦ sugar free
♦ nut free
♦ not suitable for freezing

350 g/12 oz plain white flour
¾ teaspoon baking powder
pinch of salt
1–2 teaspoons toasted
cumin seeds
200 ml/7 fl oz plain yoghurt

This is an easy recipe, great for adults but also for children to make and cook themselves. The quantity here makes 8, but it is easy to double or treble the amount if catering for a big party.

◆ Combine the flour, baking powder, salt and cumin seeds in a large bowl. Stir in the yoghurt to make a soft dough. If necessary, add a little more yoghurt: the dough should be pliable but not sticky. Divide the dough into 8 portions. Knead each one briefly, then flatten into an oval shape on a lightly floured board. It is best if the dough is quite thin.

◆ Place the breads on a grill over a charcoal fire and cook for 4–5 minutes on each side or until the bread has puffed up slightly and the surface looks brown and blistered. Eat hot, spread with a little butter or serve with a dip.

# RISE AND SHINE

WHATEVER YOU ARE DOING – going out to work, getting the children to and from school, or doing the chores and shopping – a good breakfast will set you up for the day. If you don't eat, or just grab a drink, then in a couple of hours you are likely to want a snack – the 'elevenses' syndrome – and this is likely to be a high-fat high-sugar product. Recent research has shown that breakfast-eaters tend to be slimmer than those who skip this meal.

In this chapter there are some ideas for breakfasts that can be prepared and eaten very quickly, if your main priority is staying in bed until the last possible moment, as well as recipes for those mornings when you are not hurrying out – more of a brunch than a breakfast. Perhaps this might be the way to have a meal together as a family at the weekend. Many of these dishes can be eaten at other times of day. Take a look in the next chapter for some quick baking recipes, too.

### NOTES FOR YOUR STORECUPBOARD
◆

◆ Have in stock oat flakes and/or a muesli base. Make a deluxe muesli by adding dried fruit, such as sultanas, raisins or apricots, and a choice of seeds, such as sunflower seeds and pumpkin seeds.
◆ Stock a selection of dried tree fruits, such as apple, pear, apricot, prune and Hunza apricots, for making compotes.

### TIPS FOR FUSS-FREE BREAKFASTS
◆

✔ porridge is easy to make in the microwave if you want a warming start in the winter
✔ Hunza apricots (a particular variety sold whole complete with pit) can be quickly cooked in water. The apricots and the cooking liqueur are delicious
✔ make cinnamon toast: toast one side of the bread, spread the other side with butter and then sprinkle with a little brown sugar and cinnamon and toast again
✔ try French toast (pain perdu): dip thick slices of bread in seasoned beaten egg and milk, then fry on both sides
✔ bought vegetarian sausages and baked beans make a good savoury breakfast

# Sticky Fruit Salad

- ♦ gluten free
- ♦ sugar free
- ♦ nut free
- ♦ dairy free
- ♦ not suitable for freezing

125–175 g/4–6 oz block
dried dates
450–600 ml/¾–1 pint water or
mixed water and orange juice
2 oranges, peeled and segmented
1 banana, sliced
1 mango, cut into chunks
125 g/4 oz seedless green grapes

I was brought up on this fruit salad. It is a gorgeous sweet mixture with a date and orange base, reminiscent of fruit compôte. The more dates and the less liquid you use, the darker the base will be. Unlike most fruit salads, it improves with age. You can, of course, vary the fruits according to season – it works well with most fruits except perhaps the soft summer fruits such as strawberries and raspberries.

♦ Break up the dates and stew them until quite soft in the water or water and orange juice mixture. Leave until cold.

♦ Add all the fresh fruit to the date mixture. Stir carefully and chill before serving.

# My Favourite Muesli

We have four different variations of muesli at our breakfast table: I soak mine in water, my husband has his with orange juice, one of my sons likes soya milk and the other has ordinary milk. Complicated – yes! I think I get the best deal even though water doesn't sound very appetising – the secret is overnight soaking. Apart from making the muesli light and creamy, it is easy to eat as the cereal is less chewy. The quantities here are for 1 serving.

◆ Mix the oats or muesli with the water or milk. Stir in honey to taste and the orange zest. Leave to soak overnight in the refrigerator or a cool place.

◆ The following day, add the yoghurt, grated apple, chopped nuts and fruit. Eat straight away.

◆ sugar free (optional)

◆ not suitable for freezing

4 tablespoons porridge oats or favourite brand muesli

4 tablespoons water or milk

1–2 teaspoons honey (optional)

1 teaspoon grated orange zest

4 tablespoons plain yoghurt

1 apple, grated but not peeled

1 tablespoon toasted hazelnuts or almonds, chopped

a few raspberries, sliced strawberries or seedless grapes

### EXTRA CREAMY MUESLI

◆

If you find ordinary muesli a little on the chewy side, whether soaked or not, try adding a quantity of porridge oats to the mixture. This will make the muesli softer and more creamy.

# Savoury Mushrooms

♦ gluten free (topping only)
♦ sugar free
♦ nut free
♦ not suitable for freezing

50 g/2 oz butter
350 g/12 oz mushrooms,
finely sliced
1–2 teaspoons mild mustard
grated nutmeg
salt and pepper
hot buttered toast to serve

This makes a quick hot breakfast dish, light snack or high tea. You can always ring the changes with the toast by trying a crusty granary loaf or rye bread.

◆ Melt the butter in a frying pan and add the sliced mushrooms. Cook for 3–4 minutes or until fairly soft.

◆ Stir in the mustard and a good grating of nutmeg. Season well and cook for another minute. Spoon on to the toast and serve.

# American Pancakes with Apple and Cinnamon

American pancakes make a delicious breakfast with a difference. They are sweet and light, smaller and thicker than British pancakes or crêpes. If possible, serve with a good-quality maple syrup.

......

◆ Beat the milk with the butter and egg. In a separate bowl, combine the flour, baking powder, sugar and salt. Pour over the milk mixture and whisk until smooth. Don't over-whisk the batter or the pancakes won't rise so well. Stir in the apple and cinnamon.

◆ Heat a small non-stick frying pan or griddle over a moderate heat. Pour in some batter and tilt the pan to make a pancake about 10 cm/4 in across and 1 cm/½ in thick. Cook for a few minutes or until well risen and full of holes. Flip over and cook on the other side. Tip the pancake out of the pan and keep hot while you make the remaining pancakes. Serve hot.

*Illustrated overleaf (right)*

◆ nut free

◆ not suitable for freezing

125–175 ml/4–6 fl oz milk
25 g/1 oz butter, melted
1 egg
150 g/5 oz plain flour
2 teaspoons baking powder
2 tablespoons caster sugar
½ teaspoon salt
1 apple, cut into small slivers
1 teaspoon ground cinnamon

# Tofu Strawberry Smoothie

♦ gluten free
♦ nut free
♦ dairy free
♦ not suitable for freezing

1 packet silken tofu
125 g/4 oz strawberry jam
½ –1 teaspoon vanilla essence
50 g/2 oz fresh strawberries
(optional)

Silken tofu is a great base for a 'milk shake' style drink, ideal for anyone who cannot eat dairy products or who wants a low-fat starter to the day or light snack in a glass. Whilst I have used strawberries in this recipe, I make this all year round, varying the fruit according to the season. In late summer try raspberries, blackcurrants or blackberries, and for the autumn use plums or pears. Add spices such as cinnamon or nutmeg as alternative flavourings.

♦ Whizz the silken tofu with the jam and vanilla essence in a blender until smooth. Serve as it is, or stir in some sliced fresh strawberries.

*Illustrated on previous pages (left)*

# Tropical Cocktail

♦ gluten free
♦ sugar free
♦ nut free
♦ dairy free
♦ not suitable for freezing

125 g/4 oz water melon flesh
125 g/4 oz fresh pineapple flesh
125 g/4 oz seedless green grapes
sprigs of fresh mint

This is a refreshing fruit salad in a glass!

♦ Whizz the three fruits together in a blender until smooth. Chill well and serve garnished with sprigs of mint.

# Special Hot Chocolate

This delicious thickened hot chocolate mixture makes a warming drink.

♦ nut free
♦ not suitable for freezing

1–2 teaspoons cornflour
600 ml/1 pint milk
2 teaspoons cocoa powder
1–2 teaspoons sugar
15–25 g/½–1 oz good plain chocolate, roughly chopped

*To serve*
whipped cream
ground cinnamon

◆ Mix the cornflour with a little of the milk, then stir into the remaining milk. Add the cocoa, sugar and chocolate pieces. Bring the mixture to the boil, whisking frequently so that it thickens and froths. Serve hot topped with whipped cream and cinnamon.

# Elisabeth's Winter Tea

Herb teas can be delicious, especially if you leave them to infuse for a good length of time so that the flavours really develop. This simple recipe makes a hot spicy drink that will banish gloom on cold winter days.

♦ gluten free
♦ nut free
♦ dairy free
♦ not suitable for freezing

600 ml/1 pint water
1 stick cinnamon
3 cloves
orange peel or slices of root ginger (optional)
1 tea bag, either mixed fruit or rosehip
300–450 ml/½–¾ pint orange or grape juice
red wine and sugar to taste

◆ Put the water, cinnamon, cloves and orange peel or sliced ginger, if using, in a pan. Bring to the boil. Add the tea bag and let the mixture infuse off the heat for 10 minutes. Stir in the orange juice and heat through gently. Add a splash of wine and sugar, if liked. Strain into cups and drink hot.

# Banana Booster

♦ sugar free (optional)
♦ nut free
♦ not suitable for freezing

25 g/1 oz sultanas
5 tablespoons orange juice
150 ml/¼ pint plain yoghurt
1 banana
2 tablespoons wheatgerm
honey to taste

This is a vitamin- and mineral-rich mixture that can be made in minutes. It should certainly boost your energy levels for some hours.

◆ Soak the sultanas in the orange juice for 10–15 minutes. Alternatively, plump them in the microwave for 1 minute.

◆ Put the sultanas and juice in a blender and add the yoghurt, banana and wheatgerm. Blend until quite smooth. Sweeten with honey if necessary. Eat or drink.

# QUICK CAKES AND BAKING

WHENEVER I TURN OUT A BATCH OF SCONES or a tray of biscuits, I am still surprised at how quick they are to make. Modern gadgets such as hand-held electric mixers and food processors do make all the difference, as well as scales where you can weigh one ingredient on top of another in the mixing bowl. Whilst you may feel the most fuss-free way to have cakes and biscuits is to buy them, I always prefer home-made. They are cheaper, and you know exactly what has gone into them. Baking is also a very good way to get children involved with food preparation and to teach them some basics that they may not learn at school.

In this chapter there are several very simple cake recipes, made either with the all-in-one method or a wet and dry mix which is just as easy. Skip the icing if you are short of time. The cakes and biscuits can double up as a pudding or sweet ending to a meal, or they can be packed into lunch boxes or taken on picnics. I've also included a quick bread recipe and two alternatives to bread. The savoury scones work very well with home-made soups or stews and the muffins can make any breakfast seem more special.

# Iced Carrot Cake

◆ suitable for freezing
(without the icing)

Sweet and moist, this is a very easy cake to make and even easier to eat! You can serve it at tea time or as an alternative to a pudding. If you want something plainer or dairy-free, skip the icing.

250 g/8 oz wholemeal flour
1 tablespoon ground cinnamon
1 teaspoon grated nutmeg
2 teaspoons baking powder
125 g/4 oz butter or margarine
125 g/4 oz light muscovado sugar
125 g/4 oz maple syrup
250 g/8 oz carrots, finely grated
50 g/2 oz walnuts, chopped
50 g/2 oz sultanas

*For the topping*
zest of 1 orange, taken in
fine shreds
175 g/6 oz cream cheese
50 g/2 oz icing sugar, sifted

◆ Mix together the flour, spices and baking powder in a large bowl. Melt the butter or margarine with the sugar and maple syrup, then stir into the flour. Add the grated carrots, walnuts and sultanas. Mix everything thoroughly.

◆ Spoon the mixture into a well-greased 450 g/1 lb loaf tin. Bake in the oven preheated to 160°C/325°F/gas 3 for 1 hour to 1 hour 20 minutes or until firm to the touch and a skewer inserted in the centre comes out clean. Leave the cake to cool in the tin for 10 minutes, then turn out on to a cooling rack.

◆ For the topping, blanch the orange zest in boiling water for 5 minutes; drain. Beat the cream cheese with the icing sugar until smooth. Mix in the orange zest. Spread thickly over the cake. Serve in thin slices.

# Iced Picture Cake

This is a very useful all-in-one cake that takes less than 10 minutes to mix, providing you use an electric mixer. It can be served plain, but for a quick children's birthday party, it is easy to ice. Treat it then as a picture and use writing icing pens to draw on something suitable. A coloured iced picture is just as effective as a shaped cake and a great deal easier.

◆ Line a 30 x 20 cm/12 x 9 in tin with well-greased foil. Put the margarine, sugar, flour, baking powder, eggs, milk and lemon zest into a large bowl and beat well for about 2 minutes using an electric mixer. Stir in the sultanas.

◆ Spoon the mixture into the prepared tin and level the top. Bake in the oven preheated to 180°C/350°F/gas 4 for 30–35 minutes or until springy to the touch. Leave to cool. Turn out.

◆ To make the icing, mix together the lemon juice and icing sugar until smooth, adding more lemon juice if necessary so that the icing is runny. Spread over the cake and leave to set before drawing on decorative designs with writing icing pens.

♦ nut free
♦ suitable for freezing

175 g/6 oz soft margarine
175 g/6 oz golden caster sugar
250 g/8 oz wholemeal
self- raising flour
$1\frac{1}{2}$ teaspoons baking powder
3 eggs
3 tablespoons milk
grated zest from $\frac{1}{2}$ lemon
175 g/6 oz sultanas

*For the icing (optional)*
3 tablespoons lemon juice
250 g/8 oz icing sugar, sifted

# Joanne's Coconut Brownies

Brownies are traditionally made with walnuts, but this version contains coconut which makes the brownies even sweeter and more delicious. For really good results, use a good-quality chocolate. The most important thing about brownies is not to overcook them – they should be moist and almost fudge-like in consistency. Serve in small portions as they are rich.

♦ suitable for freezing

175 g/6 oz good plain chocolate
175 g/6 oz unsalted butter
4 eggs
3 teapoons vanilla essence
½ teaspoon salt
500 g/1 lb 2 oz golden granulated sugar
200 g/7 oz plain flour
125 g/4 oz desiccated coconut

◆ Melt the chocolate with the butter in the microwave, or in a bowl set over a pan of hot water. Leave to cool.

◆ Beat the eggs with the vanilla essence, salt and sugar for 8–10 minutes. Stir in the chocolate and butter mixture, then gently mix in the flour. Finally, fold in the coconut.

◆ Spoon the mixture into a greased and lined deep 23 x 33 cm (9 x 13 in) baking tray. Bake in the oven preheated to 190°C/375°F/gas 5 for 25–30 minutes or until the surface is just firm to the touch. Cool in the baking tray.

# Savoury Herb Scones

◆ sugar free
◆ nut free
◆ suitable for freezing

175 g/6 oz wholemeal flour
50 g/2 oz medium oatmeal
pinch of salt
1 tablespoon baking powder
2 teaspoons dried thyme
50 g/2 oz butter or sunflower
margarine
1 egg
150 ml/¼ pint milk

Scones are quick to make and best eaten as soon as possible. I like adding small quantities of different ingredients to the basic mixture to get a variety of flavours and textures. Serve the scones with plain butter, or butter mixed with chopped walnuts.

◆ Combine the flour, oatmeal, salt, baking powder and thyme in a bowl. Rub in the fat. Beat the egg in a measuring jug and add enough milk to make 200 ml/7 fl oz. Pour this over the dry ingredients and quickly mix to a soft dough. Knead lightly, then roll out to 1.5 cm/½ in thick.Using a 2.5 cm/1 in round cutter, cut out scones and place on a greased baking sheet. Bake in the oven preheated to 200°C/400°F/gas 6 for 10 minutes. Cool on a wire rack.

# Cup Muffins

These are very easy, plain muffins, quick to make and bake in 20 minutes. They are ideal for a special breakfast or brunch as well as being useful for lunch box snacks. Using a cup or mug can be a very quick way to measure out ingredients. If you do not have purpose-made cup measures holding 250ml (8 fl oz), then find a suitable cup or mug that holds that amount and use it as your measure. Guess by eye whether it is quarter or half full – this recipe will stand a little inaccuracy.

♦ nut free
♦ suitable for freezing

250 g/8 oz or 2 cups wholemeal flour
125 g/4 oz or ½ cup soft brown sugar
2 teaspoons baking powder
¼ teaspoon salt
1 teaspoon mixed spice
1 egg, beaten
250 ml/8 fl oz or 1 cup milk
50 g/2 oz or ¼ cup melted butter, or 50 ml/2 fl oz or ¼ cup sunflower oil

♦ Mix together the flour, sugar, baking powder, salt and spice. In a jug, mix together the egg, milk and melted butter or oil. Add the wet ingredients to the dry ones and mix just until combined. Spoon the mixture into 12 muffin or deep bun tins. Bake in the oven preheated to 200°C/400°F/gas 6 for 20 minutes.

**Variations**
♦ Once you have got familiar with the basic mixture, you can try many variations. Add ingredients such as bran or oats to replace a little of the flour. Add chopped nuts or dried fruits such as dates or sultanas, or fresh fruits such as blueberries. Change the sweetening to use honey or molasses.

*Illustrated overleaf*

# Soda bread

◆ sugar free
◆ nut free
◆ suitable for freezing

350 g/12 oz wholemeal flour
125 g/4 oz plain flour
1 teaspoon baking powder
½ teaspoon salt
300 ml/½ pint milk
1 egg

Soda bread is a quick, simple bread that can be made, cooked and eaten in less than an hour. Many variations are possible on this basic recipe. You can add melted butter for a richer dough, or some sugar and dried fruit to make a quick tea bread.

◆ Measure the flours, baking powder and salt into a large bowl. Beat the milk and egg together and pour over the flour. Mix until you have a soft but not sloppy dough.

◆ Knead very lightly, just enough to shape into a rough ball. Put on a floured baking sheet and flatten out to a circle about 3.5 cm (1½ inches) thick. Using a floured knife, mark the dough into quarters with deep cuts that go almost through the dough but not quite. Make shallower cuts in between so that you have 8 divisions.

◆ Bake at 190°C/375°F/gas 5 for 35–40 minutes or until the crust is well browned. Cool on a wire rack.

# DESSERTS AND TREATS

This selection of my favourite easy desserts includes recipes for all seasons of the year. Some, such as an irresistible dried fruit and nut crumble, are more heavyweight for those cold gloomy months, whilst others are lighter for spring and summer. You'll also find one that is virtually sugar-free (Layered Peach and Strawberry Dessert, page 188), so you can eat a pudding without feeling too guilty if you are watching your weight.

The easiest and healthiest choice is, of course, fresh fruit. Try to make the most of seasonal varieties as well as trying different types of each fruit. Enjoy the fruit plain or try one of the fuss-free ideas on the right.

TIPS FOR FUSS-FREE FRUIT DESSERTS
◆

✔ brush fruit with softened butter and sprinkle with sugar, then sizzle under a really hot grill for 2–3 minutes
✔ purée strawberries or raspberries with a little liqueur and cream to make an instant fruit fool
✔ top and tail gooseberries and cook with a little water until split. Mash in the pan with a potato masher and add sugar to taste. Cool, then stir in some double cream
✔ sprinkle sliced bananas with sugar and lemon juice and cook in the microwave
✔ choose different coloured melons, scoop into balls and thread on wooden skewers
✔ spoon marmalade into a cored cooking apple and cook in the microwave
✔ mix honey with a thick plain Greek yoghurt and sprinkle with crunchy cereal or chopped nuts
✔ melt chocolate in the microwave and whizz with silken tofu or fromage frais for a chocolate mousse
✔ serve ice cream with melted chocolate for a rich dessert, or with some of the ginger syrup from the recipe on page 183
✔ treat yourself to a dessert wine

# Apricot and Pecan Crumble

♦ suitable for freezing

175 g/6 oz dried
apricots, chopped
2 tablespoons marmalade
grated zest and juice of 1 orange

*For the crumble topping*
75 g/3 oz sunflower margarine
75 g/3 oz wholemeal flour
75 g/3 oz rolled oats
50 g/2 oz soft brown sugar
50 g/2 oz pecan nuts

Most dried fruit makes an excellent base for a crumble, being naturally sweet and highly nutritious. As the flavour is quite concentrated, try mixing dried fruit with fresh fruit or, as in this recipe, with marmalade which gives a marvellous tang. Crumble toppings can range from a simple oats and flour mix to more adventurous ones containing nuts or spices.

◆ Put the apricots in a saucepan, pour over enough hot water to cover and leave to soak for 3–4 hours.

◆ Bring the apricots to the boil in the soaking water, then cover and cook for 20 minutes. The apricots should be fairly soft. Mix in the marmalade and orange zest and juice. Put the mixture into a greased ovenproof dish. Add a little more water if necessary so the fruit is moistened.

◆ To make the crumble topping, rub the margarine into the flour, then add the oats and sugar. Reserve 8 pecan nut halves and chop the rest coarsely. Add these to the mixture. Sprinkle the crumble topping on the fruit. Arrange the whole pecan nuts on top.

◆ Bake the crumble in the oven preheated to 180°C/350°F/gas 4 for 20–25 minutes. Serve hot.

# Pavlova with Winter Fruits in Ginger Syrup

Pavlova is like a large plate-sized meringue with a sticky inside. It is often served as a summer dessert, but I think it works just as well with some of the exotic fruits on sale at Christmas. Just to counter-act any winter chills, I like to marinate the fruit in a warming ginger syrup before piling them on to the meringue base. The quantity of syrup made here is ample for the recipe. Keep the surplus and use it as a quick topping for ice-cream or serve drizzled over pancakes.

♦ To make the meringue, beat the egg whites with the salt and cream of tartar until stiff. Add the sugar 1 teaspoon at a time, whisking in well. Then beat in the cornflour and vinegar.
Pile the meringue on to a piece of baking parchment to make a 20 cm/8 in circle. Make an indentation in the centre. Bake in the oven preheated to 140°C/275°F/gas 1 for about 2 hours. It is quite hard to tell when the meringue is cooked. If you are unsure, leave it undisturbed in the cooling oven. Leave to cool completely.

♦ For the ginger syrup, gently heat the sugar and water until the sugar has dissolved. Bring to the boil, then add the stem ginger and simmer for 2 minutes. Leave to cool.

♦ Toss the fruit in a little of the ginger syrup. Whip the cream and spoon into the indentation in the meringue. Cover with the fruit.

♦ Leave for an hour or so before serving.

♦ nut free
♦ not suitable for freezing

2 ripe mangoes, chopped
125 g/4 oz fresh dates, stoned
and chopped
1 star fruit, sliced
300 ml/½ pint double cream

*For the meringue*
3 egg whites
pinch of salt
¼ teaspoon cream of tartar
175 g/6 oz golden caster sugar
1 tablespoon cornflour
1½ teaspoons white
wine vinegar

*For the ginger syrup*
25 g/1 oz granulated sugar
150 ml/¼ pint water
2 pieces of stem ginger
in syrup, sliced

# Pear Brûlée

♦ gluten free
♦ nut free
♦ not suitable for freezing

700 g/1½ lb ripe pears
juice of ½ lemon
2–3 tablespoons sugar

*For the custard*
4 egg yolks
25 g/1 oz caster sugar
½ teaspoon vanilla essence
300 ml/½ pint cream
250 g/8 oz fromage frais

*For the caramel*
125 g/4 oz golden
granulated sugar
4 tablespoons water

These are individual rich custards with a fruit base and caramelised topping. The fromage frais gives the mixture the taste and consistency of cheesecake, denser than traditional crème brûlée but equally delicious. This will make 4–6 puddings.

♦ Peel and core the pears and chop coarsely. Cook very gently with the lemon juice, covering the fruit with a butter paper. When soft, mash roughly with a fork, adding sugar to taste. Divide the mixture among 4–6 buttered ramekin dishes.

♦ To make the custard, beat the egg yolks with the sugar and vanilla essence. Heat the cream until almost boiling, then stir into the egg yolk mixture. Add the fromage frais and mix well. Divide the custard among the ramekin dishes.

♦ Place the dishes in a baking tray and pour boiling water round them to come up to the level of the custard. Bake in the oven preheated to 150°C/300°F/gas 2 for 30–35 minutes or until the custard has just set.

♦ For the caramelised topping, dissolve the sugar in the water, then bring to the boil and boil vigorously until the mixture darkens. This takes about 5 minutes. Pour quickly over the custard and leave to set. Serve chilled.

**A QUICK TIP**

♦

If you are short of time, make a cheat's caramelised topping: sprinkle the ramekins with brown sugar and then place under a hot grill until the sugar melts and caramelises.

# Ricotta Cheesecake with Caramelised Plums

This recipe proves that cheesecakes don't have to be a million calories a mouthful to be mouth-watering. The combination of ricotta and yoghurt with a little sweetening makes a delicious topping for a simple base. Do remember to make this well in advance as it takes a day to set. As an alternative to plums, try caramelising nectarines or peaches.

◆ nut free
◆ not suitable for freezing

*For the base*
75 g/3 oz wholemeal flour
75 g/3 oz oat flakes
50 g/2 oz golden caster sugar
75 g/3 oz butter

◆ For the base, combine the flour, oats and sugar in a large bowl. Melt the butter, then pour over the dry ingredients and mix well. Press into the base of a lined 20 cm/8 in springform cake tin. Bake in the oven preheated to 180°C/350°F/gas 4 for 20 minutes. Leave to cool.

◆ To make the filling, beat the ricotta with the yoghurt and honey until very smooth. Add the vanilla essence and lemon zest. Taste and adjust the sweetening, if necessary. Spoon the topping over the cooled base and chill for at least 24 hours to set.

◆ To make the topping, slice the plums very finely and spread out in one layer on a baking sheet. Mix together the melted butter and lemon juice and brush or drizzle over the sliced fruit, then sprinkle with demerara sugar. Grill until the sugar melts and bubbles. Leave to cool. Arrange the fruit slices over the cheesecake before serving.

*For the filling*
250 g/8 oz ricotta
200 g/7 oz strained plain
Greek yoghurt
1–2 tablespoons clear honey
½ teaspoon vanilla essence
grated zest of 1 lemon

*For the topping*
3–4 ripe plums
5–10 g/¼–½ oz butter, melted
few drops of lemon juice
2–3 teaspoons demerara sugar

*Illustrated overleaf*

# Layered Peach and Strawberry Dessert

♦ not suitable for freezing

75 g/3 oz hazelnuts
75 g/3 oz medium oatmeal
300 ml/½ pint plain yoghurt or a
mixture of yoghurt and
crème fraîche
1–2 tablespoons honey or
maple syrup
2 ripe peaches, cut in thin slices
250 g/8 oz strawberries, sliced,
plus a few whole ones to garnish

This is a very attractive pudding and one which I occasionally enjoy for breakfast! Vary the fruits according to the season – it works just as well with nectarines, plums and grapes.

♦ Toast the hazelnuts in the oven preheated to 200°C/400°F/gas 6 for 6 minutes. Leave to cool, then rub off the skins. Grind the nuts finely.

♦ Toast the oatmeal on a baking tray in the oven for 5–7 minutes or until lightly browned. Mix with the hazelnuts. Mix the yoghurt with the honey or maple syrup and stir into the hazelnut mixture. Using 4 straight-sided glasses, make alternate layers of the yoghurt and hazelnut mixture with peach and strawberry slices.

♦ Chill for at least 2 hours before serving, garnished with whole strawberries.

**An alternative**
♦ For a dairy-free version of this pudding, replace the yoghurt with silken tofu. Blend the silken tofu with the honey or maple syrup until it is smooth.

# Rich Fruit Clafoutis

This vanilla-flavoured custard speckled with a mixture of dried fruit is made in minutes using a food processor or blender. It works well as both a summer or winter pudding, making a good contrast with a warming casserole or a lighter pasta dish.

◆ To make the batter, put the flour, salt, sugar, eggs, milk and vanilla essence in a food processor or blender and process until smooth. Stir in the dried fruit and pour into a buttered ovenproof dish measuring 20 x 20 cm/8 x 8 in.

◆ Bake the clafoutis in the oven preheated to 190°C/375°F/gas 5 for 40–45 minutes or until set. As soon as you remove the pudding from the oven, dust with demerara sugar. Then leave to stand, and serve warm rather than hot.

◆ nut free
◆ not suitable for freezing

50 g/2 oz wholemeal flour
pinch of salt
25 g/1 oz golden
granulated sugar
3 eggs, beaten
600 ml/1 pint milk
4 drops of vanilla essence
175 g/6 oz mixed dried fruit
(sultanas, raisins, currants)
demerara sugar for dusting

# INDEX

Elisabeth's winter tea, 169
entertaining, 9–10

fast foods, meat-free, 15
fennel sauce with cream and saffron, 101
filo pastry, 116
flapjack, honey and raisin, 174
flour, soya, 44
fritatta, Mediterranean, 64
fritters, onion, 45
fruit, 181
  avocado and fruit salad, 60
  pavlova with winter fruits, 183
  rich fruit clafoutis, 189
  sticky fruit salad, 162
  tropical cocktail, 168

garlic, roasting, 28
gazpacho, 26
goat's cheese *see* cheese
gougère with leeks and white wine, 118
grains, 103
gratins: courgette gratin, 68
  potato gratin Agenaise, 74
green bean and sweetcorn sauté, *82–3*, 84
gumbo, pumpkin, 126

hazelnuts: asparagus with lemon and roasted
  hazelnuts, 30, *34–5*
hijiki seaweed, 79
honey and raisin flapjack, 174

iced carrot cake, 172
iced picture cake, 173
ingredients, 12
iron, 11
Italian tomato salad, 32

Joanne's coconut brownies, 175

kebabs, marinated tofu and vegetable, 156

lasagne: with mushrooms and Quorn, 88
  with roast vegetables and ricotta, 89
leeks: gougère with leeks and white wine, 118
  shredded leeks with wine and crème fraîche,
  145, *146–7*
lemon butter with herbs, 99
lentils, 53
  lentil refritos, 72
  Puy lentil salad, 61
  Puy lentils and mushrooms with red wine and
  shoyu, 129, *130–1*
  spiced dhal soup, 18
  spiced lentil and almond filo pie, 117

mangoes: cashew and mango salad, 33, *34–5*
marinade, wine and lemon, 152
mayonnaise, tofu, 38
meat substitutes, 14–15
Mediterranean fritatta, 64
menu planning, 8–9
meringue: pavlova with winter fruits, 183
Mexican salad platter, 60
microwave risotto with carrot and courgette,
  110
millet, 103
minerals, 10
miso, 78
muesli, my favourite, 163
muffins, cup, 177, *178–9*
mushrooms: courgette gratin, 68
  fresh plum tomato and mushroom sauce, 102
  hot mushrooms with goat's cheese, 65
  lasagne with Quorn and, 88
  mushroom and almond rice with chilli, 111
  Puy lentils and mushrooms with red wine and
  shoyu, 129, *130–1*
  sauté mushrooms with sherry vinegar, 49
  savoury mushrooms, 164
  spinach tagliatelle with button mushrooms
  and hazelnuts, 90
  stir-fry mushrooms with spiced tofu, 76
  stuffed field mushrooms with mozzarella, 73
  wild mushroom risotto, 109
  wild mushroom soup, 25

noodles: Chinese stir-fry with omelette and
  asparagus, 77
  stir-fry noodles with sesame and miso, 79
  stir-fry vegetables with soba, 78
nut oils, 30
nutrition, 9, 10–11

oats: honey and raisin flapjack, 174
oils, nut, 30
okra: pumpkin gumbo, 126
olives: marinated olives, 48
  olive and pepper strudels, 41, *42–3*
  roast red pepper and olive bruschetta, 46
  toasted walnut and olive dip, 154
  walnut and olive pistou, 134
omelette, Chinese stir-fry with asparagus and,
  77
onions: onion and caper bruschetta, 46
  onion and caper topping, 121, *122–3*
  onion fritters with fresh coriander dip, 45
organic food, 13–14
oriental salad, 57, *58–9*

pak choi, stir-fry marinated Quorn with water
  chestnuts and, 80

pancakes, American, with apple and
  cinnamon, 165, *166–7*
Parmesan profiteroles, 40
pasta, 87–102
pasta with sauté spinach and shallots, 93, *94–5*
pastry, 113
pâté, artichoke and goat's cheese, 29
pavlova with winter fruits, 183
peach and strawberry dessert, layered, 188
pear brûlée, 184
pecan nuts: apricot and pecan crumble, 182
peppers: artichoke and goat's cheese pâté with
  roast peppers and courgettes, 29
  olive and pepper strudels, 41, *42–3*
  red hot dip, 153
  red pepper, tomato and tofu soup, 24, *138–9*
  roast red pepper and olive bruschetta, 46
  yellow pepper and caper spread, 50
pesto, 85
  couscous with, 140
pies: chestnut pie with herbs, 115
  spiced lentil and almond filo pie, 117
  Stilton and courgette strudel, 116
pilaff: cashew and saffron, 104
  sweet and sharp bulgar, 105
pizzas, 113
  crisp wholemeal pizza with herbs, 119, *122–3*
  luxury deep pan pizza, 120, *122–3*
  onion and caper topping for, 121
  rough tomato sauce for, 121
  wholemeal mini pizzas, 124
planning menus and meals, 8–9
plums: ricotta cheesecake with caramelised
  plums, 185, *186–7*
polenta: deep-fried, 97
  with roast chilli sauce, *94–5*, 96
popovers, individual cheese, 66
potatoes: baked potatoes, 142
  goat's cheese and asparagus salad with new
  potatoes and salsa verde, 54
  potato gratin Agenaise, 74
  potato wedges baked with herbs, 47
profiteroles, Parmesan, 40
protein, 10
pumpkin gumbo, 126
pumpkin seed and avocado spread, 52
Puy lentil salad, 61
Puy lentils and mushrooms with red wine and
  shoyu, 129, *130–1*

quiche, spinach and feta, 114
quick red cabbage, 150
Quorn, 15
  Cajun Quorn and rice, 108
  lasagne with mushrooms and, 88
  Quorn casserole, 133